I Dream of A New America

Keys to Reclaiming the Heart & Soul of Our Nation

By George Cappannelli

ISBN: 1-893157-24-5
13 digit: 978-189315724-8

Published by: Bridger House Publishers

P.O. Box 2208, Carson City, NV 89702, USA

1-800-729-4131

Cover design and layout: Julie Melton, therighttype.com

Printed in the United States of America
10 9 8 7 6 5 4 3 2 1

*"You never change things
by fighting existing reality.
To change something,
build a new model
that makes the existing
model obsolete."*

— Buckminster Fuller

Dedication

Although I have a reasonable amount of experience as an author, artist, entrepreneur and consultant in both the public and private sectors, including time spent as a campaign manager and special advisor in the political arena, I believe my most essential qualifications for writing this book are that I am a student of history, a citizen of these United States and I am disturbed and deeply saddened by the dysfunction and disharmony present within this nation at this time in our history. I am also disheartened by the lack of effective and intelligent action being taken by our leaders in addressing the root causes of the challenges we face and, of particular concern, by the absence of genuine compassion and conscience they demonstrate. As a result I believe that unless you and I and millions of our fellow citizens take some new and much more courageous and effective action and do so quickly, we the people, democracy as a form of government, and the rest of humanity will suffer even more serious consequences.

So I dedicate this book to you in the hope that these thoughts and recommendations – some of which you may consider realistic and practical and others more radical – will add to the public debate and prompt you to take a more active part in reclaiming the sovereignty and legacy of this great nation.

I do not claim these recommendations cover all of the necessary ground or provide all of the specifics required to chart a new course. This, I believe, is a task that should involve all of us including the very best and brightest minds and hearts, not only in this country, but from around the world. I also hope these recommendations will encourage you to get more involved in the process of self-governance and therefore become more able to participate in national and global governance. For I believe the steps we take individually and collectively today and in the coming years will determine whether we continue this rapid and precipitous decline toward the end of a noble dream or regain our sanity and once again set this ship of state on a heading that will lead us toward a proud and positive future. I believe, in fact, that it is time to begin the next and most necessary stage of the American Revolution.

Before beginning this book, I invite you to turn to Page 211. There, in succession, you will find copies of The Declaration of Independence, The Constitution of The United States (Page 217) and The Bill of Rights (Page 237). If it has been a while since you have read these documents, or if you have never read them, I believe you will find they are particularly instructive and inspiring, and of course, relevant to this conversation about our future.

George Cappannelli
Santa Fe, New Mexico
January 2008

Table of Contents

Prologue

—๛—

*I dream of a new America rising from the ashes of fear
and distrust that cloud our landscape and blind us to our
humanity, our decency and our true destiny; a new
America in which we have the courage to move beyond
half-hearted, band-aid solutions born out of compromise
and destined to fail and instead find the will to redefine
our priorities, redirect our resources, recommit our talents,
and revitalize our values so that we can realize the promise
of a democracy in which all human beings are treated
as equals and where there really is liberty, justice and
opportunity for all; a new America in which we can step
proudly and boldly forward once again into the fresh air of
hope and the sunshine of unlimited possibility to model a
new tomorrow for ourselves and for the world at large.*

*I dream of a united America in which we set aside our
divisions and stop squandering our precious energies
and resources in acrimonious public debate and biased
political positioning; a land in which we remember that
communication is about connecting, understanding and
finding commonality and not about protecting and
defending tired old illusions and false assumptions; a land
in which we refuse to sacrifice our fundamental values on
the altar of winning at any cost; a united America in
which we stop settling for the mediocre in products and*

services and for minimal advances against our most serious challenges; a united America in which we revitalize our sense of pride and purpose and recommit genuine creativity and innovation in place of the reactive strategies, limiting beliefs and false posturings that have marked our recent past.

I dream of a strong America in which wisdom, ethical leadership and diplomacy serve as our primary instruments in our quest for true alliance with others, here at home and abroad; a land in which we demonstrate to the rest of the world the futility of war and aggression; a strong America in which divisiveness and fear are not used by those who we elect to confuse and manipulate us; a land in which distortion, lies and exaggerations are replaced in the public discourse by truth, accountability, understanding, mutual respect and genuine cooperation for the common good.

I dream of a righteous America in which we take full responsibility for those who we ask to serve and who, as a result, are placed in harms way; a land in which when we are forced to defend ourselves we do so only after adequate planning, with sufficient equipment and enough infrastructure to support and nurture our defenders not only while they are away, but when they return; a new America in which we only go to war as a very last resort and then only when it is unavoidable, morally right and supported by solid evidence and the good judgment of our friends and allies.

I dream of a noble America in which we heal the wounds that encumber our present, stain our past and that stand in the way of an uncompromised future, the wounds of subjugation visited upon the indigenous people who occupied this land before us, the wounds of enslavement of our black and brown brothers and sisters who were brought here against their will, the unhealed wounds that continue to separate North from South, one religious sect from another and historic immigrant minorities from more recent ones; a noble America in which we retake the moral high ground by rekindling the promise of the land of the free and the home of the brave; a land in which we welcome those who seek refuge from oppression and limitation and allow them, through their own sweat and talent, to seek the promise of new opportunity and to contribute to our future.

I dream of a courageous America in which we move beyond the hypocrisy that has us identify our critical problems and then bury all hope of finding genuine solutions under the guise of an economic reality that masks the greed and gluttony of the few; a courageous America in which we move past the politics of scarcity into an age of abundance, generosity and gratitude; a land in which our elected officials remember that they are our servants and not our masters and where our corporations understand they too only exist to serve us and that their quest for profit is only valid if their products and services contribute to the advancement of our way of life.

I dream of a visionary America in which what we export is our wisdom, experience, indomitable ingenuity, and spirit to people around the world; a land in which we model for them a higher level of consciousness which holds that none among us is free until all of us are free and that none among us is secure until all of us are fed, clothed, given shelter and opportunity; a visionary America in which we remember and honor our democratic system, the values on which this nation was founded and the courage our forefathers demonstrated in their effort to end unfair taxation and oppression.

I dream of a compassionate America in which healthcare is not the privilege of some, but the right of all; a land in which we spend at least as much time, energy and money preventing disease and illness as we do trying to diagnose and cure it; a land in which seniors do not have to slowly descend into lives of isolation and neglect and end their days in medical warehouses, but instead are nurtured and supported in their twilight years with quality lifecare and opportunities to live and die with dignity; a compassionate America in which we take advantage of the wisdom of our elders – gathered from both their stumbles as well as their victories – and apply it for the betterment of all.

I dream of a competent America in which a genuine recommitment to excellence and quality once again constitutes the watermark against which every company measures their success; a land in which we do not have to buy special product insurance to make up for shoddy workmanship, and that the insurance we do buy actually insures our health, our lives and our property; a land in which executive and shareholder greed is replaced by genuine responsibility, accountability and a heartfelt pride of service; a land in which rightsizing is measured not against some arbitrary bottom line, but against the ability of an organization to truly serve the well being of its customers; a competent America in which all government agencies, private enterprises and not-for-profit organizations have only one standard by which they gauge their effectiveness – their ability to serve the public good.

I dream of a wise America in which the well-being of our habitat and of all the species that reside here is not viewed as a public relations opportunity by politicians or an inconvenient truth that interferes with business as usual, but instead as the sacred responsibility and trust of every citizen and business even if it means sacrificing levels of comfort and profit; a wise America in which we abandon the madness of using environmentally destructive energy sources whose purchase promotes war and aggression, weakens our economy and provides other nations with the funds to purchase American companies; a wise America in which the indisputable interconnectedness between all members of humanity and all other species that reside on this planet is used as the basis against which we measure all of our actions and the validity of our policies.

I dream of a discerning America in which we celebrate and benefit from our advances in science and technology, but do not become blind slaves to them; a land in which we have the forethought to test the impact of new products and innovations not just for their short term economic gain, but against their long term effects on human health and the environment; a land in which we base our future on forms of energy that are natural and sustainable; a discerning America in which we celebrate art and culture as well as commerce, separate journalism from voyeurism and entertainment, so called economic necessity from the public good; a new America in which we contribute our talent and labor as responsible members of this society for the betterment of our families and the advancement of our individual and collective lives and not in blind servitude to the false god of economic greed.

I dream of a enlightened America in which we serve our young, not by pacifying them with trivial pursuits, poisoning them with junk food or inducting them into mental slavery to insipid forms of entertainment, addictive video games and the emulation of celebrities and athletes who flaunt their precious gifts and degrade our primary values; an enlightened America in which we inspire and motivate our children to explore lifestyles in which their only defense against boredom is not deeper emersion in gluttonous consumption; a land in which we provide our young with quality education in life skills, core values and the arts, and offer them inspiring roles models from whom they can learn to master the art of living sane and sustainable lives; an enlightened America in which when we create programs like 'no child left behind' we are doing more than coining a politically convenient catch phrase, but are actually committing ourselves to invest all of the necessary time, energy and resources in these young hearts and minds who are our best and only hope for advancing the highest goals for the future.

I dream of a conscious America in which we celebrate integrity and champion each person's right to live a life of meaning and purpose; a land in which we reclaim our self-respect and pride not through the domination of others but as the natural byproduct of everyday thoughts, words, and deeds that align with our best and highest values; a conscious America in which all of our citizens understand the privilege and practice responsible participation in governance and who can be assured that it is their participation and not the decision of a politically appointed and philosophically biased court that will determine their future.

Yes, I dream of a new America, undivided, visionary, optimistic, imaginative, talented, compassionate, abundant, authentic, strong, committed to genuine ethical leadership, solving critical challenges and maximizing opportunities for all of the world's citizens; a new America in which we will continue the revolution begun by our forefathers and, in close collaboration with people all across the planet, finally turn this landscape of fear, distrust and scarcity into a genuine Garden of Eden.
I dream of a new America, will you dream with me?

—m—

Chapter One
Moving Beyond Fear and Distrust

—⁓—

"Once the people become inattentive
to the public affairs,
you and I, and Congress and Assemblies,
Judges and Governors,
shall all become wolves."

— Thomas Jefferson

We have lived far too long in this time of anguish and confusion, separated from each other and from ourselves by the virus of fear and distrust. Indeed, this virus appears to have become the weapon of choice in the 21st Century for so many political candidates, corporate executives, church leaders and elected officials who seem intent on using it against us as often as possible for their own narrow purposes. This virus is also spread by the media, that once proud Fourth Estate that has sold its journalistic integrity to special interests and abdicated its role as society's watchdog to curry favor with its corporate sponsors. And it is propagated and spread by many of us who, through our addiction to gossip, negativity and our willingness to accept voyeurism as news and entertainment, have allowed the public debate to be turned into a carnival side show complete with barkers, conmen and clowns.

It is this virus that contributes significantly, I believe, to the division between nations and between religious and political groups. It is this virus that separates one race from another, one economic level from the next, brother from brother, man from woman and man and woman from themselves. Red and Blue, Black, White and Brown are some of the colors the disease takes here in America, but there are other colors and other titles as well. Elsewhere in the world the colors and names may be older and more entrenched, but frankly, it does not matter. What matters is the pain and suffering, the misunderstanding, anger, bloodshed and the seemingly unbridgeable fissures that have opened between members of the human family as a result of it.

Of course, there are those among us who do not mind these fissures and who benefit from this pain, suffering and confusion. In fact, on their watch and as a result of their beliefs and actions these divides have widened. But this is not a new phenomenon. The history of the world is full of examples of rulers and despots, both religious and secular, who have advanced economic, social, political and religious philosophies that spread dissension, misdirection, distrust and fear as a means of gaining and maintaining control over what have been called, 'the masses.' How better to control humanity than to characterize the many as formless, unconscious, uneducated and dangerous and thereby to imply that the few are elevated and entitled.

What is surprising, however, is that in this so called 'Modern Age,' this Information – Digital Communications Age, such old, fraudulent and transparent practices as these that issue from limited, abusive and power driven motives should still find such solid footing. But unfortunately they do. In fact, recent history – particularly in this country – demonstrates all too well the enormous power this virus has over the minds and hearts of our people.

Creating Real Change

So what can we do about this sorry state of affairs? In this and the following chapters I will do my best to present a number of recommendations – some are more moderate and therefore would be easier to put into place while others are more radical and would be well served by additional analysis.

As I said in the dedication, I do not claim these thoughts and recommendations cover all of the necessary ground, nor do I suggest that I have all of the answers or that I am the only one who has answers. There are already enough people in the public arena today who are foolish enough to make such patently absurd and inaccurate claims.

In short, I make no attempt to duplicate the efforts of so many candidates for public office and elected officials who today put forward clearly inadequate, but detailed plans that contain only those ideas they and a relatively small group of like-minded advisors can articulate. Instead the ideas you will find here are designed to contribute to what I hope will be a much broader and more in-depth national dialogue that I believe must take into consideration the wisdom and expertise of the best, most conscious and brightest among us from all stakeholder groups as well as the hopes, dreams and aspirations of all citizens concerned about this essential and necessary task of re-charting a sane and sustainable course for the future.

All of these recommendations – even the ones you may consider radical – do, however, find their justification in the essential documents in which our founders articulated the beliefs and values which serve as the cornerstones of this nation. As a result I believe they are worth your time and consideration. Indeed, in times of challenge – and these times certainly qualify – I believe we owe it to ourselves and to future generations to have the courage to look reality in the eye, to identify what is not working and to sift through the widest possible range of alternative strategies to find solutions to the challenges we face.

I also believe we must face one unalterable and unavoidable fact – we cannot get to the new and genuine solutions we so desperately need by continuing to think and act on the same level and using the same values and processes that have served as the soil from which these problems have sprouted. No, our values have been abused and distorted not only by those without genuine compassion and conscience who claim to lead us, but also by those of us who call ourselves citizens. As for the soil of our political process, it has been polluted for too long by the corrupt and dispirited who have abused it for their own selfish ends and compromised by those of us who, by tuning out and turning away, have given them permission.

Nor do I believe we can fix the enormous challenges we face with band-aid solutions so weakened at birth by compromise and weighed down with pork barrel encumbrances that they are bound to fail. And we certainly cannot pretend that we can treat the issues that confound and obstruct our progress as separate – energy, healthcare, education, environment, poverty, disease, immigration, foreign relations, etc. – and pretend to work on them one at a time. No, these issues are interrelated and interdependent.

Instead I firmly believe we must follow Albert Einstein's sage advice – to find genuine solutions to the problems we face we need to have the courage and discernment to go to a higher level – a level of higher values and more conscious actions – and from this place seek new solutions, 'whole systems' solutions that address our problems at causative levels. Surely that, in the end, is what a free society, a noble and courageous society, a democratic society must do – we must continually elevate and refine our game to stay true to the vision and mission of our forefathers.

Taking Our First Step

To this end, I believe our first and most important job as citizens of this democracy – a job that is clearly identified and encouraged in the opening paragraphs of our own Declaration of Independence and in the quote by Thomas Jefferson that opens this chapter – is to send the bums packing! Yes, as an essential step in opening up the public dialogue to the fresh air and sunshine of genuine inquiry and to the search for real solutions and new alternatives, we need to take responsibility for our government back by getting rid of the dangerous, intellectually challenged, arrogantly insensitive, unresponsive power hungry reactionaries who have a strangle hold on the executive branch as well as those timid, ineffective, political chameleons on both sides of the aisle in our Congress and within our Judicial branch and those pompous poseurs in the media who are colluding with them. I mean, seriously, in a land as powerful, diverse, talented and remarkable as this, are we so naive and disheartened that we miss the danger to democracy posed by this crowd of bullies and political thugs? In a land as extraordinary as this is this crop of sub-par elected and appointed officials and media meddlers really the best we can do?

It is both sad and ironic to me that we spent millions of dollars, more than two years of our time, zillions of kilowatt hours of media and public attention and many thousands of hours of valuable Congressional focus trying to impeach a president who created a reasonably stable and respected administration – respected both here and abroad – and who helped us engineer one of the most prosperous periods in our history because he demonstrated the poor personal judgment to have sex with a younger woman. ("Let him who is without sin – with either women or men – cast the first stone.")

In turn, we have allowed those who clearly lack both the skill and intellect to lead, those who fabricate information and misdirect the public, Congress and our allies; illegally invade other nations; send thousands of American servicemen and women to their deaths, violate both the spirit and the letter of the law of our Constitution; allow their cronies and patrons to openly pillage some of our most valuable and diminishing natural resources; sanction the violation of the Geneva Convention, refuse to participate in the Kyoto Accord, contribute to escalating global acrimony and the rise of terrorism; place us in great danger by barely acknowledging global warming and intentionally architect the largest run up of national debt in our history in just six years, a national debt that now exceeds the debt accrued by all other presidents in U.S. history combined, to continue unscathed in office simply because they claim to be Christians and posture as 'good old boys.' Truly amazing! This current gang of unconscious incompetents in the White House, Congress and the courts make Warren G. Harding and his crowd (undoubtedly, until now, the worst president and administration in American History) look like rank amateurs and the Tea Pot Dome Scandal appear to be reasonably benign child's play.

So our first order of business and the best thing we can do for the health and well-being of America, in my opinion, is to show those on both sides of the aisle and in the media who are ineffective and humanistically challenged – and there are many – the door. At least, that is what we should do while there is still a semblance of the light of democracy still burning. And if the current Congressional quagmire will not allow impeachment or if the process of culling them from the Judiciary and Legislative branches itself will require too much of our critical national focus, we should take matters into our own hands and reclaim our government before it is too late. For as Cicero said, *"No power is strong enough to be if it labors under the weight of fear."*

What are the grounds for showing them the door? In the case of the incompetents who have pretended to lead us in the latter part of the 20th and thus far in the 21st Century, I identified a number of the reasons a couple of paragraphs back. But these are only the surface effects issuing from a much deeper cause. The fact is we live in a representative democracy, a republic. It is a form of government in which *'supreme power resides in a body of citizens entitled to vote and is exercised by elected officers and representatives responsible to them and governing according to the law.'* It is a form of government in which each citizen gets to cast their vote not on each and every legislative and constitutional issue, but instead to elect individuals who are supposed to have the capacity and desire to serve as our representatives in this legislative process.

It has been – at least until recently – a reasonably decent system and certainly a substantial cut above tyranny and oligarchy, but it requires one essential ingredient to be successful, a social contract and sacred trust between those of us who vote and those of us who are elected as our representatives. This social contract also requires that our representatives when acting on our behalf carry out our intent and uphold both the spirit and the letter of our Declaration of Independence, our Constitution and our Bill of Rights. Indeed, it is the reason we elected them.

Henry David Thoreau described the situation this way. *"There will never be a really free and enlightened state until the state comes to recognize the individual as a higher and independent power from which all of its own power and authority are derived and treats him accordingly."*

Unfortunately these under-performing, under-qualified, unresponsive, egotistical and self-serving individuals who populate Washington and a number of state and city capitals as well as the members of our media seem to have forgotten this social contract and sacred trust. Instead – based on their track record – they appear to believe they were elected not to represent our will, but to execute their own personal agendas. They appear to believe that elections are some kind of periodic inconvenience they have to endure in order to allow them to have the freedom to do whatever they want the rest of the time. They appear to believe that our job as citizens ends once the ballots are counted (legally or not) and from then on they have the right to do pretty much whatever they want with our natural resources, with our money, with the lives of our young people and with our fundamental principles and values. And so, from my perspective, this gross abuse of their offices and our trust constitutes more than adequate grounds for their immediate dismissal.

Remember our Declaration of Independence tells us – *'Governments are instituted among Men, deriving their just power from the consent of the governed.'* Remember we live in what is supposed to be a representative democracy and a republic not an oligarchy or monarchy.

Focusing On How, Not If

How do we show them the door? Every citizen who is troubled by the state of the state should make it their daily practice to flood the White House, Congress and the Supreme Court with letters, emails and phone calls demanding their resignation and not stop until we have their complete and undivided attention. We should also stop making any and all financial contributions to both political parties and to all candidates until politicians on both sides of the aisle remember that they exist at our pleasure and they start demonstrating the ability and willingness to make the kind of serious changes that are needed.

We should turn off the national financial faucet by threatening and, if necessary, executing a tax-withholding revolt until whoever is our President as well as the members of Congress and the Judiciary remember that they work for us and that the money they are squandering on their own narrow personal agendas is our money. We should ensure, through our communications and our votes, that any and every Senator or Congressman in both parties who wants to be elected or re-elected understands, in no uncertain terms, that their continued ineffectiveness and support for these arrogant and reactionary policies will eliminate their future chances for elected or appointed office.

We should also boycott our daily news programs and stop buying the newspapers and magazines we read until the media comes to its senses and agrees to again provide us with accurate, honest, unbiased and in-depth reporting on the stories and topics we need to know about. Indeed, we should deny them an audience and all revenues until they come to their senses and start doing their job. And in case they do not remember what that job is, it is reporting, not interpreting, spinning, censoring, biasing, gossiping and reducing our public debate to trivialized entertainment for their own and their sponsor's gains.

In short, we should do everything in our power, including making the ultimate sacrifice of taking to the streets in the next phase of the American Revolution, to let this and any future leadership in Washington and those who collude with them or are afraid to oppose them know that they have violated our trust and the spirit of this democracy, and that we will no longer stand for it. For as a bumper sticker I saw recently suggests – *"Never have so few taken so much from so many for so long."*

And least you call my recommendations absurd, illegal or un-American, I direct your attention to a quote by Daniel Webster – *"The contest for ages has been to rescue liberty from the grasp of executive power;"* and to more than a few essential thoughts contained in our Declaration of Independence. And please do yourself, your family, your children and this nation a service by reading these words again slowly and reflecting on them rather than passing over them as you and I have done so many times before.

> *"...When in the Course of human events, it becomes necessary for one people to dissolve the political bands which have connected them with another, and to assume among the powers of the earth, the separate and equal station to which the Laws of Nature and of Nature's God entitle them, a decent respect to the opinions of mankind requires that they should declare the causes which impel them to the separation.*

> *We hold these truths to be self-evident, that all men are created equal, that they are endowed by their Creator with certain unalienable Rights, that among these are Life, Liberty and the pursuit of Happiness. — That to secure these rights, Governments are instituted among Men, deriving their just powers from the consent of the governed, — That whenever any Form of Government becomes destructive of these ends, it is the Right of the People to alter or to abolish it, and to institute new*

Government, laying its foundation on such principles and organizing its powers in such form, as to them shall seem most likely to effect their Safety and Happiness. Prudence, indeed, will dictate that Governments long established should not be changed for light and transient causes; and accordingly all experience hath shewn, that mankind are more disposed to suffer, while evils are sufferable, than to right themselves by abolishing the forms to which they are accustomed. But when a long train of abuses and usurpations, pursuing invariably the same Object evinces a design to reduce them under absolute Despotism, it is their right, it is their duty, to throw off such Government, and to provide new Guards for their future security."

Chapter Two
Redefining Leadership & More

—◊—

"Nearly all men can stand adversity,
but if you want to test a man's character
give him power."

— Abraham Lincoln

At the same time that we are showing this crop of incompetent, ineffective, arrogant and unresponsive elected officials and appointees the door and silencing the media voices that manipulate us, we have to change the way we identify and evaluate those who wish to run for and hold public office, now and in the future. The rigorous use of emotional intelligence, psychological and drug testing as well as in-depth background checks should be a prerequisite for all candidates for all public offices at all levels.

These are, after all, the minimum requirements for employment at many levels in most organizations in the public sector and even in many government agencies. So why not insist on their use to measure if our candidates for public office have strong enough values, high enough levels of intellect, stable enough emotional foundations, effective enough communication skills and demonstrated abilities to serve the greater good? We do, after all, want the best of the best to lead us, don't we?

We must also require and be prepared to engage in a new form of genuine, open, honest public debate on the real challenges we face in all election campaigns from the local to the national level rather than settling for the insipid, manufactured, managed, cosmetic interactions that occur today during political campaigns? We deserve to know and should demand to know what our candidates really know, believe and stand for and what they will do once elected. And one of the best ways to learn this is to reduce or eliminate the role played by the political mercenaries who have co-opted our election process. In short we should get all of the middlemen, ad men, handlers, spin doctors, media coaches, self proclaimed tea leaf readers and others who believe their job is to manipulate the electorate out from between the candidates and ourselves as citizens and voters so that we can find out who these candidates really are and whether they are capable of representing us and serving the greater good.

In instances where candidates duck issues during a campaign or obscure and hide their beliefs behind clever words and slogans, we should not expect these individuals to do any differently once in office. Where candidates engage in political disinformation, character assassinations and similar negative strategies, we should be clear that they will do no less with and to us once elected. What's that old Chinese aphorism – *'actions create habits, habits create character and character creates destiny.'*

Educating Our Leaders

We should create a number of special universities and schools where individuals who wish to pursue public careers must go to learn how to lead; where they are required to participate in programs that introduce them to the lessons of history and to fully explore the moral and ethical duties of candidates for public office and for elected and appointed officials as well. Yes, just as we have military academies to train our military leaders, medical schools for our doctors, law schools for our attorneys, we should have enough political and public service schools to ensure that all who want to represent our interests receive an enlightened education in the art of compassionate and noble leadership. And no one, and I mean no one, should be elected to or appointed to a public office who does not graduate with a credible record of performance from one of these schools.

The bottom line is that we have to re-evaluate and refine the standards we use to evaluate our candidates and office holders. The time for cronyism, nepotism, and the overwhelming importance of money, family connection, willingness or physical appearance as the primary qualifications for leadership should be declared over. The time when psychologically unbalanced or emotionally immature individuals should be able to act out their inferiority complexes and personal wounding on our nation and on the world should be brought to an immediate close. The time when we expect individuals to have all of the answers and we accept their obsessive focus on task (the what) rather than on process (the how) should also end. These are inadequate, invalid and dangerous litmus tests for effective public service.

Instead we must require demonstrated capability, in-depth training, a quality education in the arts and humanities as well as commerce, a wise and discerning mind and an awakened heart to become the pre-requisites for those who wish to serve. And I call your special attention to the word 'serve.' For as John Andrew Holmes said, *"There is no exercise better for the heart than reaching down and lifting people up."*

In short, we need to do everything in our power to ensure that those who represent us – and I remind you that we live in a representative democracy – and who are charged with serving our needs, crafting our laws, spending our money, protecting our resources and who have within their power the ability to commit us to war or to architect peace are well qualified to do so.

We do not need a 'superman' or 'superwoman' to save us, we need representatives with genuine conscience, high enough values, enough humility, and sufficient heart and intellect to participate in guiding the process that contributes to our *'safety and happiness.'*

Limiting Special Interests

We also need to do all that we can to limit the excessive influence special interest groups and multi-national corporations have upon these candidates and office holders. And this will require a lot more than enacting tepid campaign finance laws and pointing our finger at 'corporations' and 'lobbyists' as the only source of the problem. It will require that we reverse the degradation and undermining of our basic values that we are all colluding in. It will require that we remember the social contract and sacred trust that is essential for the practice of democracy.

We must also have the courage and honesty to look to the real root of this problem and admit that the exercise of excessive influence actually begins with each of us who belong to a group or organization that tries to purchase influence from our political candidates and elected officials. Indeed, as anyone who has ever been involved in or close to a political campaign knows this is where the problem begins. Before we write a personal check, or the development officer or fund raiser (bagman) of the organization we belong to delivers the money (payoff) to the candidate – and it does not matter whether the organization is benign or malevolent, in favor of left handed dog walkers, greater freedom for the pharmaceutical industry or unlimited power for the gun control folks – we and our bagmen want assurances the candidate will advance our special interests once elected. In short, to limit the excessive influence of special interest groups and multi-national corporations each of us who represents or is a member of one of these special interests or is an employee or stockholder in one of these corporations must stop condoning and contributing to the purchase of our candidates and elected officials. Only when we recognize that it is our efforts to buy our representatives, our desire to gain unique advantage and to short-circuit the public debate that ultimately undercuts democracy, will the ship right itself. No wonder so many of our candidates and office holders are for sale, we have trained them to sell themselves and punish those who do not.

We also need to demand truth in advertising and limit the amount of it as well as the size and form of political donations that support it. No matter how many logical arguments are advanced regarding the challenges of reaching voters in the modern world, the real truth is that the plethora of communications tools available in this Information Age, if used by candidates with integrity, honesty, competency and decency, are more than sufficient to reach the hearts and minds of every man, woman and child in the world.

Creating A Level Playing Field

If we go further and finally level the playing field by crafting and enforcing real laws on campaign financing and campaign spending and provide all candidates with an equal, realistic and limited amount of free media time, we can return the election process to sanity. And sanity is clearly lacking. What else can one say about a process that allows and requires a group of candidates for the Presidency to spend almost a billion dollars collectively on one race? It is insanity! Indeed, it is insane to turn both our election and legislative processes into fund raising circuses and auctions that not only eliminate many of the most highly qualified candidates from running, but also ensure that only those with questionable values and with chameleon like qualities rise to the top.

It is also patently absurd and destructive to our interests to require those we elect, especially at the national level, to spend most of their time once elected raising funds needed for re-election rather than attending to their legislative duties and responsibilities. (For example, the average U.S. Senator, even from a moderately sized state, must raise about $25,000 dollars a day every day they are in office for six years in order to have sufficient money to underwrite their re-election campaign under our current system. Our President must raise two or three times that amount each day for re-election and as a result must literally start running for re-election the minute he or she enters office – a situation that clearly interferes with and biases every legislative decision and initiative.

The bottom line is that our election and campaign funding processes are broken and we must fix them along with a number of other things that have contributed substantially to subverting the democratic process and we must fix them immediately if we are to save this nation from decline.

Cleaning Up and Clearing Out the Media

I have already mentioned the wholesale sell out of the media, so I will not spend much time on that aspect of the topic. However, until and unless we put stringent ownership guidelines in place that ensure an independent media, and until we require our journalists, reporters and so called news commentators to demonstrate the highest level of integrity and decency, neutrality and accuracy in providing us with in-depth and unbiased reporting, our democracy will remain at risk. Surely, even the most unconscious members of the Fourth Estate know that this patently absurd attempt to entertain and manipulate us rather than educate and inform us is both demeaning and destructive. Surely, even the most indifferent among us as citizens recognize that the media has lost its way. All of this obsessive and misleading focus on events and conditions – many of which are meaningless – and all this strutting about and puffing up on public stages as if they as reporters and commentators were entitled to be the seers of the Information Age obscure the fundamental fact that it is the media's job to report and it is our job to take in what should be neutral, in-depth information and then make intelligent and discerning decisions for ourselves. No one gave the media permission to decide things for us. No one asked them to step outside the boundaries of their profession and present themselves as authorities in some new world order. We must put an end to these practices and do so now!

Celebrating Democracy

In other countries where democracy has either not yet taken root or taken root only in distorted models, we must do all that we can to ensure that truth and information about democracy and alternative models of government and constructive strategies reaches the hearts and minds of the people through every and all avenues. And in doing so we must have patience and trust in the wisdom that Oliver Wendell Homes, one of our greatest legal scholars, shared with us. *"In the free marketplace of ideas truth always triumphs."*

We should also restrict the participation of representatives from these oppressive and uncooperative nations to the role of observers rather than as voting members on governing councils in world bodies. And we should boycott the goods and services these countries produce – even if we loose business opportunities or have to do without some things – until such time as they take genuine steps to enter the human family with responsibility and decency. No matter what arguments our economic gurus and business lobbyists advance, the long term and detrimental cost to us of financing the activities of these governments with our trade and investment dollars as well as our foreign aid, far out weigh any immediate gains. Indeed, one need only look closely at the enormous and almost over-whelming challenges we face today as a result of our willing-ness to kneel to the gods of fossil fuel to verify this contention. Conversely, one need only consider what would happen if we – collectively with all other nations of conscience – were will-ing to suffer the short term consequences of boycotting our purchases from these nations.

To this same end we should also limit the ability of our gov-ernment to support these regimes with aid packages ensuring that the only aid we give them is verifiable humanitarian aid.

We should not, however, isolate the people or the leaders of these governments from interaction with the world – as we have with Cuba and other nations – but instead we should welcome them into a genuine dialogue as often as possible, a dialogue in which we admit our own frailties and explore the means by which we and they can elevate our goals; a dia-logue in which we do all in our power to understand their unique challenges and needs, to offer alternatives to their assumptions and misunderstandings and to assist and encour-age them to join the interdependent human family. And where none of these methods prove successful, we should work in genuine concert with other nations to exert all other necessary and constructive influences possible to get their attention and prompt them to redirect their energies.

I am not so naïve or ignorant about the way the world works or about the motives of those who are more focused on the desire for power and domination than on the common good to believe that these recommendations are, in any way, easy to implement or that they will be quick in coming. Long standing divisions, entrenched positions of power, habituated behaviors, reliance on greed and corruption, legacies of hatred and distrust, the wounds from past grievances and aggressions, the stranglehold money and privilege have on many governments and institutions, the seemingly innate fear of what is different, centuries of patterned responses, malicious intent and, of course, our insufficient skill at utilizing genuine cooperation and collaboration rather than war as the instruments to achieve our objectives make this a very long and challenging uphill road. But if there ever was something worth fighting for, this is it! If there was ever a challenge worthy of our ingenuity and capacity, noble and far reaching and essential enough to warrant our focus, this surely is it!

Focusing on the Power of One

The nature and complexity of this challenge is also the principal reason I believe that, in the end, the single greatest and most powerful antidote we have against the virus of fear and distrust whether sown by our government, our media, our corporations, or our religious institutions is our personal willingness to raise the level of our individual consciousness and to start demonstrating mature behaviors that are aligned with our most treasured values. For in the end, we must first learn to exercise self-governance before we can hope to participate in systems of collective governance.

Unfortunately, in this 'Aspirin Culture' where we have been numbed into unconsciousness and become accustomed to avoiding discomfort at all costs through our overuse and reliance on medications, food, sex, entertainment, overwork and overplay, this task of raising our individual consciousness and demonstrating behaviors that align with our most treasured values is, of course, not an easy thing, and, as a result, is something far too many of us avoid.

Unfortunately, however, if we continue along this path much longer, I believe our capacity for genuine action may well be lost. So we have to stop self-medicating and wake up from this bad dream. We have to remember that unconsciousness and numbness are in direct opposition to our desire for self-governance. We have to remember that self-governance is the only arena in which each of us has any real and immediate impact and direct control. We must remember that raising the level of our consciousness is the only arena in which we can practice without permission or the need for outside resources and the only arena through which we can ever gain enough momentum to eventually make the sort of collective, communal, regional, national, and global changes that are necessary to ensure a truly sane and sustainable world.

How do we wake up? Where do we begin? Wherever we are! How do we begin? First and foremost by being honest with ourselves and admitting that we have been asleep; that 'we' and not some faceless 'they' are ultimately responsible for the state of the state; that our frailties and follies are at the root of our biggest challenges. We must admit that we need to better understand our mis-steps and our mis-deeds in order to identify and evaluate the strengths, skills, resources and opportunities we need to capitalize on going forward. In short, we must recognize that we are human, that we have stepped off the path and that, as La Rochefoucauld reminded us, *"Almost all of our faults are more pardonable than the methods we resort to hide them."*

So in addition to demanding much more of our current leaders and being much more discerning and wise about how we qualify our future leaders, we must also demand much more of ourselves. We must be courageously honest about our motives and our means and, over time, learn to bring our thoughts, words and actions – and most especially our addiction to self-numbing behaviors – under control and into alignment with our highest values – the values we claim as our own in church on Sunday mornings, the values we communicate to our children as they grow-up, the values we know in our hearts to be right.

We must also ensure that truth is the primary currency each and every one of us spends and requires in every area of our daily lives – in our families, at work, in our communities, in our churches, schools, clubs and organizations. If we practice truth in these areas, eventually we will find that truth becomes the main currency we all exchange all across our nation and in the world at large.

Understanding the Difference Between Power vs. Force

To get to this goal we must certainly improve the quality, reach and content of our news, information and especially our education – and not just for children, but for citizens of all ages. Only through education, education that invites, informs, stimulates and empowers, can we raise our own consciousness to a high enough level where the cheap and negative tricks and mental gymnastics that pass as public debate; where the habituated and destructive behaviors as well as the lies, distortions and exaggerations that have become common practice at all levels of our culture are seen for what they are – attempts to manipulate and mislead us and to undercut our democratic process by aggregating power in the hands of the few.

Yes, if we are ever to find ways to immunize us to both the short and long term effects of the diseases of misunderstanding, manipulation and malevolence which issue from these viruses of fear and distrust, each of us as citizens must wake up and work to attune ourselves to what Dr. David Hawkins in *Power vs. Force* has identified as the frequencies of courage, willingness, acceptance, reason, love and joy.

Much easier said than done, of course! To be successful in raising our individual and then eventually our collective consciousness we must redefine our priorities, revisit a number of the limiting primary beliefs we hold about 'others,' learn to accept ideas and actions that are different from our own, judge a lot less, accept and trust a lot more and, above all, learn to be curious about what we do not know and those we do not understand. Only by exercising such acceptance and curiosity can we ever understand the motives and needs of others and thereby put ourselves in a position to neutralize destructive tendencies and address genuine needs – our own and theirs.

We must also be willing to sacrifice some of our comforts and let go of habituated behaviors that have us focused so exclusively on self-gratification and material acquisition (self-numbing) and instead shift our attention to contributing a lot more time, energy, skill, resources, attention and willingness to the common good. Indeed, we must, as Lester Levinson, a former mentor of mine, once said, "Want truth and higher consciousness, the way a drowning man wants air."

Literally, to be successful in immunizing ourselves against the virus of fear and distrust we must want our freedom, decency, honor and the well-being of all of humanity above all lesser goals. We would also be wise to remember that we are all in this together and that as the old African proverb tells us, *"If you want to go quickly, go alone. If you want to go far, go together."*

Rooting Out Hatred and Violence

Individually and jointly we must also stop supporting those religions, political parties, and social, fraternal and community organizations that foster and spread the message of separation; that disparage and condemn those who are different and who are so narrow in their focus and short of vision that they create environments that are the breeding ground for ignorance, hatred, divisiveness, isolation and violence.

We must also shine the light of truth on religious leaders who claim to represent the Divine, but who instead abuse their sacred trust by distorting the precepts of their faiths and thereby contribute to this climate of fear and distrust. Indeed, to be successful in raising our level of consciousness as a nation we must be particularly vigilant in publicly discrediting religious leaders who play upon our need for guidance as a means of spreading falsehoods and distortions that suggest that some of God's children are more deserving or entitled to His love and grace than others. We must recognize as Jonathan Swift once said, *"We have just enough religion to make us hate, but not enough to make us love one another."*

In the political, social, and economic sectors, where the distortions are sometimes harder to see because the motives of those who perpetrate them are hidden under the guise of overly obtuse theories and philosophical arguments, we must exercise greater discernment. In these sectors where secular leaders abuse our need for guidance and their sacred trust by playing upon our most basic fears – security, safety and control – they should be called out and then run out of town. This calling out is one of the jobs our media has abdicated. The running out of town is one of the jobs we, the people, have abdicated.

What are some other antidotes to these poisons? When each of us admits to ourselves that no amount of wishing or hoping for a better government or a more enlightened leadership will ever produce them and that no level of material accumulation or financial wealth will ever bring us genuine security, safety and control or protect us from the things we ultimately fear the most – loss of loved ones, disease, emotional pain and death – the attempts by the greedy, the gluttonous and the power hungry to manipulate us will be seen for what they are – the slights of hand of the unethical who want to obscure their baser motives for their own gain.

Are these the only or even the best antidotes and recommendations? Absolutely not! The ways to counter the virus of fear and distrust are as limitless as the scope of our individual and collective imaginations and the depth of our willingness to know the truth and live according to the fundamental principles our hearts tell us are right and just. The one essential factor, however, that must be present for these and other antidotes to work, is our genuine desire to get out of our heads long enough to reconnect with our hearts and through this reconnection to live according to our essential spiritual values – the values that our founding fathers referred to as *'the Laws of Nature and of Nature's God.'* Only in this way can we wash away the ashes that cloud our vision and allow our natural desire for the bright and beautiful light of a new day to be satisfied.

Indeed, when each of us chooses to value our dignity and freedom most highly, to practice integrity, reclaim our sovereignty and do the essential individual work of raising our consciousness; when each of us commits to participate actively and intelligently in determining our own destiny and in reclaiming our democracy; when each of us demands of ourselves and others the best that we have to offer, we will have begun to take the next and the best steps on the path to curing the disease of fear and distrust. We will also have begun the next phase of The American Revolution.

So let us be courageous enough and patient enough to conduct a new kind of public and private discourse. Let us commit to bringing greater diligence and discernment to our search for real solutions and greater vigilance to the process of identifying, electing and then monitoring our leaders. Let us commit to the individual and personal work necessary to regain our balance and realign our thoughts, words and deeds with the natural laws of harmony. Let us also remember that without our investment in these qualities and practices we will continue to be played and played badly by those who are willing to sacrifice the greater good for their self-serving personal agendas. Let us remember that without our investment in these qualities and practices we will continue to squander this most precious gift called democracy and all of the promises it holds for the well-being of humanity.

Chapter Three
Redefining Priorities, Re-vitalizing Values

—⚏—

"Nothing doth more hurt in a state
than that cunning men pass for wise."

— Francis Bacon

In order to create a truly sane and sustainable world, I believe we must do a lot more than tweak the inadequate, politically compromised and minimally effective strategies we are currently pursuing in the areas of education, ecological sustainability, healthcare, lifecare, energy, international diplomacy, human rights, immigration, defense and many other essential areas. This approach is clearly not working. And, if we believe experts in our psychiatric professions, it is dangerous for anyone to keep doing the same thing over and over again and expecting different results. Indeed this is, we are told, one of the first signs of insanity.

Instead I believe we must redefine our priorities, redirect our resources, re-commit our talents, and revitalize our values so that we can realize the promise of a democracy in which all human beings are treated as equals and where there truly is liberty, justice and opportunity for all.

Yes, nothing less than a full and thorough overhaul of the American way is needed. As Buckminster Fuller, noted architect and visionary, said about overhauls. "You never change things by fighting the existing reality," he said. "To change something, build a new model that makes the existing model obsolete."

This is not to imply that everything about our way of life and our current model is wrong or broken. Clearly there are many extraordinary and remarkable things about life here in America, things that millions of us and billions of individuals in other parts of this planet desire, admire and respect. This does not, however, mean that it would do us any harm if the things that are working as well as the many other less than extraordinary, unremarkable and broken policies, practices and structures we have created were evaluated with new eyes and altered with open hearts and discerning minds.

To accomplish this re-evaluation we have some well-honed methods at our disposal. For example, from time to time, organizations in the public sector that are in financial jeopardy or have suffered serious leadership challenges require that all of their people re-apply for their jobs. On the surface this may appear to be a somewhat odd requirement, but upon closer examination, I believe you will discover this process gains a lot of purchase and value.

The re-application process prompts people at all levels from those at the top to those who are the most recent new hires to re-examine their qualifications and behaviors, evaluate their responsibilities and contributions, revisit policies, procedures and structures, recalibrate their effectiveness, and in this way, contribute to renewing and refreshing every aspect of the organization. In short, this process provides the opportunity to shine the bright light of truth on habituated behaviors, limited thinking and ineffective and unproductive processes. It brings fresh ideas, new energy, higher degrees of productivity and performance, much greater honesty and healthy and positive competition into what was previously a closed, habituated and failing system.

Re-Envisioning America

So what do you think would happen, if every American was required to do precisely this on a regular basis? What would happen if every man and woman involved in government – and that includes the President, Vice President, members of Congress and the Judiciary, appointees and civil servants – had to reapply for their jobs every year while in office and not just every two to four to six years when they are up for re-election? And what if this reapplication process was not only conducted as a self-evaluation in front of the electorate or their constituents but before panels of their peers selected from all stakeholder groups and parties?

What do you think would happen if each of them had to re-examine their effectiveness and the value of their contribution and report to us on the results of this reapplication and on their commitment to improve in areas that require it?

And what would happen if they used this process to retune and recommit to higher standards and we used this process as a baseline for gauging their performance in the year going forward?

What do you think would happen if we joined with these legislators in re-examining the laws that are on the books for their relevance, for possible bias and for inequity? What would happen if we revisited our Constitution regularly, not with an eye to dissembling this remarkable document, but to refining it and making it even more extraordinary and relevant to the challenges and opportunities of the current age?

What do you think would happen if each company and organization in the public sector required its owners, managers and employees to re-apply for their jobs and used this process to re-invent themselves and the organization itself – not just at their launch or when mergers, acquisitions or financial failures occur, but on a regular basis? What would happen if we asked each company to revisit all of their products and services, policies and systems, visions and values on a regular basis with the same discerning eye?

What do you think would happen if every non-profit organization did the same thing? If each school, church, community, fraternal and social organization and family did as well? What would happen if we took our collective and individual visions, goals and objectives and revisited them with an eye toward making our lives, our communities, our organizations, our nation and our world better?

If we follow Buckminster Fuller's sage advice and 'build a new model that makes the existing model obsolete;' if we take advantage of Albert Einstein's suggestion that 'we cannot solve the problems we have created by continuing to seek their solution on the same level on which we have created the problems,' then it becomes clear that continuing to do what we are currently doing is not only insufficient, it is bound to fail. Instead we must do much more, do much better and do much that is different. We must literally re-envision America and all of our working parts. And we must then use this new vision as the benchmark as we re-visit our priorities.

In the process we must do our best to identify the dynamics that are at play in countries thousands of miles from our shores and determine if they are as high a priority as the quality of our own education, the state of our healthcare, the integrity of our news and information services, the effectiveness of our technology, the quality of our lifecare, and the stability of our primary institutions. Get it? We must honestly evaluate our resources, how we utilize them and determine if they are assisting us to develop systems and practices that truly improve the quality of life of our citizens so that we, in turn, can contribute our knowledge and energy to assisting others around the world to do the same.

We must start remembering – as the old Chinese adage advises us – 'the journey of a thousand miles begins beneath our feet.'

Weighing Results Against Rights

We must also ask ourselves if our habitual and sometimes unthinking support for a specific political party or a particular leader or our support for a specific category of individual rights is more important than the well being of the tenants of our democratic way of life. This is, after all, not some sports contest or game. We are not the fans and our politicians are not players on a field or court. This is real! This is life! This is our life! This is our country!

We must also decide other critical things. Is the protection of the right to accumulate huge amounts of profit by multi-national companies under a free market economy more important to our way of life than the protection of the environment or the health of our citizens? Is the right of the individual to bear arms (especially semi-automatic weapons) and our right to privacy (especially the privacy of those with emotional, psychological and criminal histories) more important to us than the right of our citizens to live in safety? Is the right to accumulate unlimited personal wealth more important than the ability of our society to take care of the needs of those who by virtue of poverty, lack of education, cultural biases or norms, histories of physical or emotional abuse, physical incapacity, and other limiting factors, cannot take care of themselves? Is the protection of some of our intellectual and real property rights and patents on areas of (God given) knowledge more consequential than providing seniors or children and the underprivileged with the kinds of services and medicines they require? In short, how much is enough and can we not employ our imagination, creativity and talent in the cause of finding the right balance between protecting the rights of the individual and advancing the well-being of humanity?

Not easy questions, these! Indeed, they go to the heart of what we call democracy. And yet if we really want to find our way out of the quagmire of confusion we now find ourselves in; if we really want to stop our precipitous decline as a nation, then I believe we must address these and many more questions with much greater honesty and integrity than we have demonstrated in a very long time – perhaps in fact since those courageous future citizens gathered to draft the foundational documents on which this nation rests.

A re-envisioning such as the one described here at all levels all across this nation will, I believe, greatly assist us to rediscover our path toward a strong and sustainable future. It will also assist us in determining what new resources we need, what talents need to be developed, what new skills need to be honed and how we might actually cooperate with and learn from those who already have some of these skills and talents that can serve our collective needs.

This re-envisioning will also assist us in revisiting our core values and deciding whether or not they are the values we want to champion and, if so, what we need do to retune and revitalize them and encourage their practice and integration at all levels of our culture.

I realize, of course, that there will be many who will call this a foolish and impractical concept. I can hear already here their comments. *"What are we supposed to do, shut down the whole country while we do this re-envisioning?" "It will slow us down and interfere with our economy." "In this climate of division, it would be an impossible task." "It's impractical and naïve!"*

Well, I say, nonsense to all of that! A genuine re-envisioning is possible and can be done relatively quickly and effectively without ruining our economy or stopping us in our tracks. I say we can do it in scalable ways while we go on with our daily lives. All that it takes is our genuine willingness and commitment to learn and to improve. All that it takes is our commitment to observe, identify and then change the things we see that are not working. All that it takes is the application of our enormous energy and ingenuity to making America healthy and strong and balanced again.

A genuine re-envisioning is also not just possible, but necessary. Not just necessary but essential and authorized. Indeed, according to principles established in our Declaration of Independence it is both our privilege and right to do this. Remember – *"That to secure these rights, Governments are instituted among Men, deriving their just powers from the consent of the governed, – That whenever any Form of Government becomes destructive of these ends, it is the Right of the People to alter or to abolish it, and to institute new Government, laying its foundation on such principles and organizing its powers in such form, as to them shall seem most likely to effect their Safety and Happiness."*

Will this re-envisioning bring about challenges and raise obstacles that are unexpected? You can count on it! Will it take time? You bet! But if we approach this re-envisioning with the right intention, if we implement this re-envisioning on individual and then local levels first – in our own lives, in our companies, in our local communities and governments; if we focus on the smaller and more immediate challenges before tackling the larger and more national and global ones, then we will not only gain experience and confidence in the process, we will also gather momentum, passion, and energy along the way that will assist us to get the job done at higher and broader levels. Remember, the first law of improved performance is to do small things consistently in strategic places.

If we keep this law in mind and allow our hearts as well as our minds to lead us, we will find that we will eventually incorporate this kind of continuous improvement model into everything we do everyday and in this way, the task of envisioning will be a regular and relatively easy occurrence.

In the end, of course, the real question is – Do we have a choice? For those who are comfortable with the current state of the state; who believe that this steady downhill slide toward chaos and dysfunction is either not happening or acceptable; who believe it is their divine right to grab as much of everything as they can for themselves, the answer will, of course, be to leave things alone and let this system and those who are currently working it to their advantage have free rein.

For those of us who recognize that we are on a collision course with our destiny, however, the answer will be a resounding – No! We do not have a choice. We must start doing things differently and for different reasons now. Only in this way can we produce different and much more constructive results. Only in this way can we demonstrate true sanity. For to continue to do the same things over and over and expect a different result is, as I said earlier, one of the first and truest signs of insanity.

Chapter Four
Rediscovering the Fresh Air of Hope

—⚊—

"What makes greatness is starting
something that lives after you."

— Ralph Sockman

If we have the courage, patience and discipline to pass through this re-envisioning process, (and not just once, but on a continuing basis) we will, I believe, be taking our next and best step back into the fresh air of new hope and unlimited possibility. We will also be earning the right to reside in the desirable space of continuous improvement, and be gaining enough wisdom in the process to be able to regain our footing when we slip. Finally, of course, we will be demonstrating our right to lead others. Yes, through this continual process of re-envisioning we can identify and then put down many of the limited behaviors and constricting beliefs that today are derailing us.

What will we find in the fresh air? Renewed energy, enhanced self-confidence, greater creativity, improved productivity, a resurgence of self-confidence, increased innovation, and more. Why? Because these are the automatic rewards that come to those who take the time to re-chart their course, align their actions with their values, redefine their roles and responsibilities and commit their resources and talents to worthy and meaningful goals. I want to stress that these are not accidental outcomes. They are automatic rewards.

What other benefits will we find in this sunshine and fresh air? We will again turn toward the promise of a democracy in which all human beings are treated as equals and where there really is liberty, justice and opportunity for all. While this may seem to some to be fanciful and unrealistic as a goal, especially in this age of cynicism and doubt, it is anything but. With closer scrutiny, I believe you will find that these and other fundamental values on which this nation was founded have served as the essential fuel that propelled it, especially during its formative years, to levels of unprecedented growth and prosperity. In fact, while some of the cynics and power mongers might call this a romantic, impractical goal it actually fulfills the prerequisite for growth and well being that Carl Jung, the noted psychiatrist and one of the founding fathers of the Science of Psychology, articulated a number of years ago. When asked to identify the reason some of his patients achieved major breakthroughs while others did not, he said that in his experience those who achieved genuine breakthroughs were driven by a secret they would not or could not communicate. It was this secret that fueled those who overcame the obstacles and impediments that obstructed others.

In the case of America, I believe our secret fuel has been our core values and guiding principles and the more we again commit to steer our ship of state by them, the more easily and swiftly we will cover the distance between this dangerous, erratic, undisciplined and shabby present and a new and extraordinary future; between this period in which we are experiencing a significant and rapid decline in our values, a diminishment in our self-respect and in the respect in which we are held abroad and the instability of many of our primary institutions and the extraordinary opportunity and promise contained within our Constitution and our Bill of Rights.

The truth is, we do not have another sane and sensible choice. We can take up the challenge of cleaning up the mess we have either created or allowed others to create or we can stand by mutely and witness the further decline of one of the greatest nations and one of the most noble, human experiments in governance in the history of the world.

Gauging the Tipping Point

How close are we to the tipping point? I believe we are only one election away from either an unalterable decline or from the start of our resurgence. Indeed, I believe that if we have the requisite courage and awareness, we will send this band of power hungry, regressive, selfish, small-minded, fear mongering elected officials packing and replace them with those who can actually assist us in refocusing our future. But we cannot be naïve or deceive ourselves with fantasies about some man or a woman on a white horse who will save us. In this time of crisis, we are the only ones who can save ourselves!

We cannot, of course, be naïve about the fact that making the kinds of change I am talking about will not be easy, especially in this age in which our media has become a tool manipulated by government and owned and supported by corporate sponsors rather than the source of trustworthy independent reporting. Nor can we rely on the abilities or largess of new leaders alone. Instead we must be willing to take responsibility for our own governance and at the first sign of deviation from the desired path by our leaders and representatives we must exercise the full weight of our influence.

Revisiting Checks and Balances

What else can we do? Reform our government. The system of checks and balances is broken and in dire need of repair. It has always been tested, but recently it has been violated by a band of school yard bullies and meglomaniacs who have distorted both its spirit and intent. We must also find a way to curb the powers of the president. It is now clear that no one human being, no matter how intelligent, courageous or conscious should be able to make decisions that impact not just all Americans, but all of humanity.

I do not, of course, claim to have all or perhaps even adequate solutions to these and other challenges. But I am certain that these issues deserve diligent study and input from our best, brightest and most conscious. We should also begin the search for these solutions immediately, for one thing is abundantly clear, if we do not fix what is broken and fix it soon; if we do not begin this redefining of the roles and responsibilities, and refining of systems and structures, we will loose even the tenuous footing we now have.

Before visiting a few ideas that I want to contribute to the public dialogue on restructuring, I remind you again of those words from The Declaration of Independence that both justify and require us to restructure our government – *"Governments are instituted among Men, deriving their just powers from the consent of the governed, – That whenever any Form of Government becomes destructive of these ends, it is the Right of the People to alter or to abolish it, and to institute new Government, laying its foundation on such principles and organizing its powers in such form, as to them shall seem most likely to effect their Safety and Happiness."*

Redefining the Role of the President

So here are my suggestions – redefine the role of President perhaps dividing that role between co-presidents – one for external and one for internal affairs. Or give a much more expanded role to the Vice President to accomplish this purpose. Require all members of the judiciary (especially the Supreme Court) to run for public office. Explore a new form of constitutional assembly that combines the best features of our representative democracy with the parliamentary systems that calls for ongoing votes of confidence. Establish term limits. Expand our two party system to a multiple party system that ensures an environment with much greater diversity of opinion and options. Eliminate all loopholes in the campaign finance laws, set spending limits and establish government funding of political campaigns. Provide free, equal public access to all media by all candidates for a specified period of time. Fire the army of political mercenaries, etc., etc.

The possibilities are endless and we should consider as many as we can from the seemingly ridiculous to the obviously significant, for as some of the great innovators in history tell us, great ideas often seem absurd or ridiculous to the uninformed in the beginning.

Refreshing the Courts

Based on historical record, it is clear to me that the question of lifetime appoints to our courts, especially the Supreme Court, needs to be revisited. Our world is too complex and the challenges and dangers too many and too far reaching to allow individual Presidents, especially those with very strong and biased political beliefs, to appoint individuals during their term in office that we are then stuck with for several decades. Originally, of course, it was thought that the interaction between the executive and legislative branches of our government would off-set this bias and help keep our system in balance, but as we discussed in the previous section, once our elected officials began disregarding both the spirit and intent of our Constitution, the system of checks and balances began to fail. Therefore, I believe it is time to consider instituting another layer of safeguard by giving citizens the right, through vote or referendum, to change the composition of our courts – particularly when there are individuals on them who serve their own beliefs more than they serve the will of the majority. I realize, of course, that this poses its own dangers, but if we believe in the value of a representative democracy, then we would be wise to consider applying it at all levels of our government and to uncovering ways to do this that protect the spirit of our Constitution and serve the greater good.

Enforcing the Separation of Church and State

What else can we do? Strictly enforce one of the primary tenants of our democratic system that our founding fathers crafted – the separation of church and state. It is time to take churches out of the business of politics. For that matter, I believe it is also time to take churches out of the business of business – especially the tax free business. They exist for the advancement of our spiritual lives, not for the purpose of accumulating wealth and abusing their power. Indeed, it is absurd that churches should be granted immunity from taxation and then allowed to use our donations and contributions to amass great wealth to influence and interfere with the political process.

It is also time to take politicians and politics out of our churches. This is not to suggest that we should forget that we are 'one nation under God indivisible with liberty and justice for all.' Rather it is to remember that in a land as diverse as this we cannot allow the beliefs of any one religious or anti-religious group to dominate our political landscape. And if elected officials do not have the intellectual capacity and moral fiber to separate their individual religious beliefs from their political decision making and leadership, we should invite them to become members of their church clergy and step aside from the business of being our duly elected representatives. While this should be true for all elected and appointed representatives, it is absolutely essential for those who occupy our highest offices.

The same is true for religious leaders. If they cannot stay out of the business of politics and the business of business, then they should be required to give up their collars and run for public office or take positions in private industry where they can accumulate the personal power and wealth they desire.

The bottom line is that democracy's only hope for survival lies in our ability and willingness to keep church and state separate and to continue to support the primary tenants on which the American Revolution was executed.

Chapter Five
Reuniting Our Divided House

—∿—

*"Every man takes the limits of his own field
of vision for the limits of the world."*

— Arthur Schopenhauer

It takes neither a genius nor an in-depth analysis of the great
books of the world to understand the old adage that 'a divided house will not stand.' Indeed, any child who has spent
even a few hours at the beach building a sand castle or used
toys or cards to build a structure has learned this truth first
hand. And yet, our nation today is terribly divided; political
parties and the religious groups that support them rail against
each other with abusive language and in ugly, acrimonious
debate that exceeds the bounds of anything that could justifi-
ably be called competition or common decency. The same is
true in so many other areas of our culture: environmentalists
vs. corporate interests; those in favor of the war in Iraq vs.
those opposed; those who support a woman's right to chose
vs. the anti-abortion crowd. Suddenly it seems that the
strategies of the schoolyard bully have become standard

operating procedure in the-anything-goes arena of contemporary politics and public life. Suddenly it seems that we have lost the ability to disagree respectfully and to treat our opponents and competitors with civility and respect. Suddenly it seems we have decided that the best way to challenge ideas that are different from our own is to call into question the character and motives of those who hold these ideas.

But please, do not confuse my outrage for naiveté. The world of power politics whether played by kings, churchmen, despots or tyrants, dimwitted or enlightened leaders has never been a timid or friendly game. Indeed, the history of power politics is full of every kind of mayhem from the outright theft of office to the incarceration of opponents, from the imposition of rigid limits on free speech to gross acts of violence and murder. Still we do not live under a Divine Right Monarchy or tyranny, but instead in what is purported to be a democratic state and so what we are seeing today – the intentional lies, the malicious character assignations, the hanging Chad shenanigans, the destruction of government files and tapes, the underhanded behavior and vicious infighting of political operatives for whom winning – at any cost – is all that matters, is unacceptable among free men.

Of course for those who believe they benefit from this division, for those who would weaken and confuse us further so that they can advance their selfish individual political and economic agendas, this political climate is not a bad thing at all. As long as neighbor is distanced from neighbor, one religious sect is made to vie against another, political parties and factions within them are duped into acrimonious debate, race is pitted against race, economic segment against economic segment, then the selfish intentions of the few will continue to hold sway over the well being of the many.

Remarkable isn't it that the negative words, thoughts and intentions of a relative few can change the mood of an entire gathering or, in this case, an entire nation? So what can we do to prevent small minded bigotry, selfishness, greed and prejudice from poisoning the well? What can we do to heal our divided house?

Acknowledging Unalienable Rights

First and foremost I ask you to remember these lines from our Declaration of Independence –

"We hold these truths to be self-evident, that all men are created equal, that they are endowed by their Creator with certain unalienable Rights, that among these are Life, Liberty and the pursuit of Happiness."

Please consider these words carefully. Please notice that our founding fathers believed *'the truths'* they identified in the Declaration of Independence were *'self-evident.'* They were not something that had to be pondered endlessly in rude and divisive debate by so-called elected representatives or interpreted by courts of politically biased and appointed legalists. They were not something that only the learned or the wealthy or the powerful or the few could understand or appreciate. They were *self-evident* to all human beings.

I also ask you to pay close attention to the term *'unalienable rights.'* Those who drafted and ratified our Declaration of Independence and then our Constitution did not believe our rights originated with the Republicans or Democrats whether conservative or liberal. They were not instituted by Executive Order nor did they require support by the Christian Right, The Catholic Church or the ACLU. No, our founders believed these *'unalienable rights are endowed by our creator.'*

So I believe it is both necessary and ultimately simple – although not necessarily easy – to prevent the few from poisoning the well of the many. And this simple although not necessarily easy work must begin with each of us. As individuals we must first work on reducing and then eventually eliminating the abusive, unkind, prejudicial thinking, speaking and acting out that occurs in our own heads and hearts. *"Strange place to begin," you say! "Sounds like Sunday School stuff."*

Well I believe it is the best and ultimately the only effective place to begin working on the issues that divide us for only in this way can we ever get to the source of the problem. Only in this way will we ever have a reasonable chance of actually reducing and eliminating the thinking, languaging and behaving that is the primary cause of our challenges.

Going to the Root of the Problem

Working on reducing and eliminating our personal propensity to practice abusive, unkind, prejudicial thinking and communication in our own lives will give us the ability, awareness and the right to work on its occurrence in our boardrooms, on production lines, in the halls of Congress, in our companies, communities, social and fraternal organizations, and in our churches. For, indeed, this kind of negative thinking and destructive, divisive schoolyard behavior has no place in the landscape of a genuinely free, morally conscious society.

And unless we put an end to this kind of thinking, speaking and acting out, and to the growing belief that it is okay to win at any cost, we run the risk of inducting future generations into this kind of behavior as we ourselves have been inducted into it by those before us. Indeed, we have the power to stop this bullshit here and now. We have it in our power not to perpetuate the 'sins of the father unto seven generations.'

How else can we put an end to the kinds of behaviors that divide us? If our elected officials demonstrate these behaviors, we must, as I said earlier, censor them and, if they continue the practice, we must vote them out of office. If the perpetrators are the political operatives who represent a particular candidate then we must require the candidate to clean up their act or we must not cast our vote for them no matter how competent we think they may be in other areas. Indeed, if divisive strategies and behaviors are happening in their name they need to be held accountable for it.

If the divisiveness is contributed to by a member of the clergy or an educator, they too should be put on notice and if it continues they should be stripped of their post. And if for some reason the hierarchy of their church or school is inclined to excuse or protect their own then we should publicly expose the situation and stop attending that church or school. Remember, in this culture we not only have the ability to vote at the ballot box, we have the ability to vote with our attendance, with our dollars and with our volunteer support.

If divisiveness is supported or sponsored by a business we should boycott their products, refuse to use their services and not purchase their stock. Remember, it is we and not they who ultimately control the state of the state and their level of success and profitability.

While this may seem excessively punitive or difficult to implement, I assure you it is neither. Unless we stamp out this kind of thinking and behavior, we run the risk of giving it even greater license and we cannot afford to do this and expect to live in a democratic society. Indeed, if we simply set the bar for public performance in government, business, religion and education higher, we will find that the natural laws that are present in our hearts will ensure our return to the sanity of civilized public debate and civilized behavior.

We will also discover something else of critical importance. We are not divided by natural law or by inherent flaws in our characters, but by the intentional and malicious manipulation of information, habituated behaviors and the distortion of truth perpetrated by some members of our species. To rediscover this we need only stop the manipulation and distortion within our own beings and we will wake up from this bad dream of a divided house.

Chapter Six
Rejecting Mediocrity, Practicing Excellence

—⁓—

"Success is often just an idea away."

— Frank Tyger

It is sad, unfortunate, but true that America has become a land in which we are now accustomed to settling for mediocrity in many of our products and services, for reduced amounts of innovation and for minimal advances against our most serious and debilitating problems. I realize that this statement will raise the ire of many who still believe that we are the best, have the best and produce the best. And yet those of us who travel to other parts of the world with any regularity know that this is simply no longer true. Indeed, it is an illusion. All across the planet there are cities rising that far exceed our own in size and services. All across the planet so called 'third world' countries are expanding at astounding rates and engaging in the economic race in powerful ways. All across the planet countries we are making rich through our purchase of their products and services are beating us at our own game and also coming back with their riches to purchase our companies in what is becoming a permanently a depressed economy.

Even those who do not travel learn this truth when they discover that only six of the top twenty-five technology companies in the world are in the U.S. or owned by U.S. interests; that many smaller countries in the world such as South Korea, Finland and Sweden invest much more in research and development than we do; and that people in South Korea and India – many of whom are excluded from our shores by highly questionable immigration practices – now apply for many times the number of patents annually than people in the U.S. Not to mention the fact that many other countries outrank us in healthcare, lifecare, longevity and education.

Americans also learn the truth about our loss of competitive advantage when we have to participate in product recalls, have our American made car or truck repaired, or have to return an electronic component or device, a cell phone or PDA made in America. We learn it when we read about advances in social and medical services in other countries. In short, we learn it when we discover that there are many nations in the world who today are producing products, offering services and experimenting with alternate life strategies that are significantly superior to our own in quality and price.

Taking A Wrong Turn

I am not sure exactly where the incredible powerhouse that was America went astray or when this lack of personal pride and commitment to excellence and innovation began to negatively impact our way of life. There was a time, indeed a time not all that long ago, when we would have been appalled at the idea that we would accept shoddy workmanship, use less than the best raw materials or resources, and settle on the passable and sub-standard as the American standard. Indeed, it would have been considered un-American at best and criminal at worst.

And yet this sorry scenario holds true not only in regard to the quality of our products, but in regard to our services as well. For example, in this 'not very long ago time' that I just referred to customers were not considered an unnecessary inconvenience on the way to accumulating greater profits, but were instead considered an integral and essential part of the process. In fact, not very long ago we still believed that customers were the reason for making the products and delivering the services in the first place. Customer response was one of the primary ways most people in our society got personal satisfaction and measured their effectiveness. We often knew our customers by name, considered them our most important asset and treated them with courtesy and respect. Remember the old adage, 'the customer is always right.'

Not anymore! Today far too many of the companies and organizations that I deal with seem to have forgotten this adage. Indeed they have lost the art of customer service to such a degree that when I come across a company that still prides itself on providing genuine service I am always a little stunned.

Instead, in most cases what I encounter when I reach out to most customer service departments are not live people devoted to providing genuine service, but extraordinarily complex, computerized voice messaging systems that do everything in their power to prevent me from talking to a live human being who might be able to actually address my issue with some semblance of courtesy and ease. Even on those occasions when I am patient enough and lucky enough to eventually wend my way through the maize of automated choices and options and actually connect with a live human being, they are so far down the decision making chain that they lack any real power to address even the simplest variation on the theme. Or worse yet, they are in some remote city in India with no authority to do anything, but to keep repeating the same inane choices over and over again. And when I try to make my way out of these closed loops and ask to speak to a senior executive in the company, my request in often met with silence. You see, most people in customer service positions today do not even have access to a company directory and so the idea of speaking directly to one of the giants who operate in the rarified atmospheres at the top is more than unusual, it's downright sacrilegious.

Of course, this brief look at service does not address the actual manufacture of products. Most American companies, even those who identify manufacturing as their primary business, have for the most part long ago distanced themselves from the actual manufacturing process itself. Instead they contract offshore for their production and, as a result, delegate responsibility for the quality, workmanship or workings of their products to others. And to make up for this delegation of responsibility they now offer us product warranties.

Funny, isn't it? Funny and sad that we, the consumer, in addition to spending rather hefty sums to purchase a product, must now buy an extended warranty to cover the high probability that it will have defects and need repairs. I am not sure whose bright idea it was to introduce these warranties, but clearly, as consumers we were not bright enough to see the sucker punch coming and so now companies have another rather large source of revenue and we are left with another bill to pay.

And like all things American, once an idea takes root, there are always those who soon figure out how to expand upon it especially where profitability is involved, so we now have a number of different kinds of warranties. We have platinum warranties and gold, silver and, of course, tough love warranties. These are the ones where you get to throw the product away and purchase another. But no matter how special or expensive the warranty or how immediate the response of the geek or goon squad, most of these extended warranties do not cover the cost of the down-time, the inconvenience, and often, the loss of business opportunity that results while the product is being repaired. No that's just part of the special privilege we get by buying the product.

Viewing the Customer As An Inconvenience

Seriously, how did we get to this sorry state of affairs where customers are an inconvenience, customer service is automated and product manufacturers are not responsible for what they make? How did go from having such pride in what we manufactured, from the willingness to stand behind it and from doing an honest days work for an honest amount of pay, to this slipshod, irresponsible, lowest common denominator, disposable product society that we now live in?

How did we get to this place where we have to buy special product insurance to make up for shoddy workmanship and cheap materials; this place where the insurance we do buy often does not insure our health, our lives or the property it promises to protect? How did America become a land in which executive and shareholder greed became so blatant and out of balance relative to the compensation and benefits provided to the workforce? How is it possible that we have arrived at this time in which we consider it normal and acceptable for executives who fail badly in their responsibilities and duties to walk away with millions of dollars in salary and bonus? How did we come to view 'rightsizing' as something to be measured against an arbitrary definition of a financial bottom line rather than against the ability of an organization to truly serve the well being of its customers? How did we arrive at this time in our history when government agencies, private enterprises and not-for-profit organizations worry more about the wrath of their shareholders or boards of directors than they do about justifying their existence based on one and only one true standard – their ability to contribute in a genuinely meaningful way to the greater public good?

I will leave additional tracking of this nation's decent down this slippery slope to mediocrity to others who are better equipped to document this troubling phenomenon. Instead, I will use the limited time we have together to look at some of the things I believe we can do to reverse this trend, and to consider what we – both individually and collectively – can to do to revitalize our sense of pride and purpose, and to use our remarkable energy, innovation, science and technology to live once again in a land in which excellence is the song we sing; in which we remember the advice given us by David O. McKay who said, *"Find a purpose in life so big it will challenge every capacity to be at your best."*

Going Beyond Commerce

Again, I do not believe the fix is anywhere near as complicated or convoluted as the strange and twisting path that brought us to this sorry state of affairs. Indeed, I think the fix begins and ends in two fundamental areas. We have to stop using commerce, material acquisition and profitability as the only measures of our success and each and every one of us must start making different choices every day in the way we do what we do in our daily lives.

If we stop believing that without profitability our world will collapse, we might actually come to realize that it is our quest for profit that blinds us to deeper realities and contributes substantially to many of the abuses we must grapple within our world. To this end we must put different standards in place by which we judge our success. Imagination, creativity, intuition, and insight have to be elevated at least as high and preferably higher than reason. We must also learn to celebrate and reward those whose work is essential to our progress of as a nation – our artists and our teachers to name just two. For any nation that forgoes its commitment to art, culture and education in favor of commerce will, in the end, lose its ability to resonate with the genuine rhythms of the soul and the beauty of the natural world.

Simultaneously, if we shift our next thought, word or deed away from accepting the mediocre, the less than, the undisciplined, the quick fix, the inferior, the impatient, selfish, shoddy, or any of the other things that lead to poor quality in products and service, we will be taking a next and very important step toward halting our decent.

If we go a step further and learn to exercise greater discernment in the products and services we accept and vote with our wallets by not buying or paying for mediocre products and inferior forms of customer service, we will take another and equally important step. For if there is one thing that gets the attention of those elevated souls who isolate themselves from the nagging army of the less advantaged beings who are their customers, it is plummeting profits.

What else can we do? If we do buy something whether it is a large something like an automobile, home appliance or a small something like a meal, office supplies, etc., and we find that it does not meet our expectations or the product's or service's announced benefits are not fulfilled, we should send or bring it back and demand a full refund – no matter what the store's or dealer's return policy may be. Like plummeting profits, truckloads of returns will certainly get people's attention.

Utilizing General Strikes

What else can we do? We should borrow the practice used so effectively in so many other places in the world, we should start executing general strikes. Yes, in masse we should declare next Tuesday or a week from Friday as 'I'm

Not Going To Take It Anymore Day' and on next Tuesday or a week from Friday we should take to the streets in protest of the products and services that are less than acceptable or we should agree on that day not to use or buy products or services that do not meet our standards for excellence in workmanship and value.

In short, we need to take our power and sovereignty back. We need to stop this lemming-like behavior that keeps sig-naling those who choose to take advantage of us that it is okay to do so. We do not, for example, have to accept woe-fully inadequate and unconscionable seating configurations on airplanes or the absence of meal service or the terrible on time arrival records or the insufficient number of pilots, air controllers or airline mechanics who as a result of overwork and insufficient rest put our lives in danger each time we fly. We do not have to allow movie theatres to bombard us with advertising when we have paid a reasonably substantial price to see a movie. We do not have to accept poor or inad-equate medical care from understaffed hospitals because there are owned by companies more interested profits than in delivering quality care. We do not have to allow organi-zations of any sort – in either the private or public sectors – to charge us for inferior work-product, goods, services or materials. We do not have to allow organizations – includ-ing our own government agencies – to treat us as if we were an inconvenience. And we certainly do not have to allow our nation to continue this slide toward becoming a 2nd or 3rd rate nation simply because we and the leaders we elect lack the vision, courage or intelligence to reverse this trend.

Using What You Make

And if raising the level of our personal commitment to excellence, returning or rejecting inferior products and services and exercising our rights through general strikes and boycotts do not do the trick, then we should enact legislation and adopt policies that require every head of every government agency and every senior executive, owner and member of a management team in every company or business in America to use their product or service on a regular basis in the same way their regular customers do. Yes, every airline executive should have to fly in coach in a middle seat at least three or four times a week – or at least until they get the message.

Every subway, bus, or taxi executive should have to use their subway, bus or taxi at rush hour and in inclement weather as their primary mode of transportation. Every road commissioner should have to drive on their roads in older cars with worn shock absorbers. Every prepared food executive should have to eat their own packaged foods every day at every meal. Every used car salesman should have to drive the cars they sell and pay for their repairs. Every legislator should be required to utilize the services and follow the processes that he or she has either voted for or against. Every judge should have to spend at least one day a month working in the prisons they sentence people to. Every attorney should have to experience being defended or prosecuted in a court of law by a court appointed attorney. Every stock broker should be required periodically and randomly to pay for the losses incurred by their clients. Every doctor should have to experience the services – including surgery – as an ordinary patient in another hospital or emergency room. And every member of Congress, of the judiciary and of the Executive Branch, and that includes the President, Vice President and members of the cabinet should be required to experience life every week from the perspective of the ordinary citizen and without the buffers and bullshit that normally surround and insulate them.

You get the picture, every individual who is responsible for every product, service and policy in America should be required to use these products, services and policies regularly and that includes working their way through their own customer service departments, warranty procedures and administrative and bureaucratic red tape.

Adopt this kind of legislation and enact these kinds of policies and watch how fast we get our act together again. Watch how quickly we Americans return our attention to excellence in performance in products and services.

Chapter Seven
Reclaiming Pride and Purpose

—⁂—

*"The price of greatness
is responsibility."*

— Winston Churchill

This question of reclaiming our personal and national sense of pride is also tied, from my perspective, directly to our ability to rediscover and reclaim meaning and purpose in our lives and to our willingness to invest courage, energy, creativity and innovation in living out that meaning and purpose on a daily basis.

To accomplish this I believe we must start 'doing' a lot more and thinking and talking about doing a lot less. Yes, we have to roll up our sleeves and re-engage in our actual lives rather than in the virtual lives far too many of us are now living. This means spending a lot less time hiding out in front of televisions and computer screens and playing video games and sports fantasy games and a lot more time out in the physical world interacting with people, participating in local organizations, donating our time and talents, learning skills, and engaging in real time activities with family and friends. And as we discussed in the previous chapter, it also means doing whatever we do – from the most ordinary and mundane task of washing a dish or making a phone call to the most complex task of conducting a relationship, raising a family, leading a church, an organization or a country – with a much greater commitment to excellence, craftsmanship and quality.

To reclaim our sense of pride I believe we also have to be willing to turn down the external noise and distractions that are present in this media mad world long enough to be able to once again tune in to our own inner wisdom. Only in the quiet can we differentiate between what we think and believe and what the world keeps telling us to think and believe. Only in the quiet can we digest this knowledge and integrate the strategies and actions that emerge from our inner wisdom into our lives. This means we have to re-engage and revalue the arts, music, culture, education, reflection, meditation and prayer as much, if not more than, commerce. We have to remember and value the simple comforts and pleasures of relating to others, enjoying a good book, a good meal, a good conversation.

For it is these practices that open our hearts and allow us to hear the 'inner wisdom' that resonates within us. It is these practices that will also allow us to rediscover our sense of purpose and meaning. An example from Carl Jung's autobiography, *Memories, Dreams and Reflections,* speaks to this. In the book he describes a visit he made to a Hopi tribe in the Southwestern United States. During his visit he noticed that even the most ordinary members of the tribe seemed to exhibit an unusually high sense of pride and dignity, much more in fact than their American and European counterparts. They moved with grace and self-confidence and seemed to exude a quiet kind of strength.

Jung was puzzled by this, but for a while could not discover the source. It was only after he had gained the confidence of the Chief that he learned that the Hopi believed that part of their mission in life was to help the sun cross the sky each day. What a mission! To help the sun cross the sky each day! No wonder they walked tall! No wonder Jung found them to be so different from their American and European counterparts!

If Jung were alive today, I'm sure he would have a lot to say about the absence of meaning and purpose in both the American and European cultures. In our case, I am sure he would point to the fact that in the early stages of this nation we gained much of our sense of pride and meaning from the principles on which our new nation was founded; on the fact that we lived in what we called 'the land of the free and the home of the brave.' Our sense of pride and purpose also came from the fact that we opened our hearts and arms to welcome others who came to our shores from less fortunate places rather than building walls and utilizing prejudice as the foundations for our immigration policies.

I'm sure Doctor Jung would point to the fact that it used to be that our sense of pride and meaning was connected to our sense of social responsibility and our willingness to share the abundance of this great nation with others around the world who were in need. I am sure he would tell us that from his perspective one of the things that made us different from others was that we believed a part of our primary mission was to model democracy and share its values with the rest of the world; a large mission indeed, one that almost rivals that of the Hopi.

Rediscovering the Source of Our Motivation

So where have all of these primary motivators gone? Clearly they did not disappear overnight, although there is little doubt that a reasonably large number of them have been sacrificed over the last several decades under the misguided watch of at least two or three significantly under skilled Presidents, a highly divided Congress, a biased Judiciary, an abdicating media and a disenfranchised populace. But no matter how limited any President's intelligence might have been or how misguided their values, no matter how much of a pawn any of them have been to corporate forces and small-minded and narrow-focused special interests, the truth is that not even a President with limited vision and his cronies can be blamed entirely for the sad state of the state we find ourselves in.

No, each of us has created, promoted or allowed this turning away from the foundational things that previously gave us a special sense of pride and purpose. Each of us is responsible for those who hold office (especially when we elect them to multiple terms) and for the shoddy state of quality in our products our services, the declining passion for public service, the disappearance of an independent media, the disinterest and withdrawal of our children from engagement in life and a whole lot more.

Yes, our leaders are certainly to blame for squandering resources and opportunities of a magnitude and at a pace unheard of in the recent history, but they do not share that burden alone. We stood on the sidelines and allowed it to happen or we contributed directly to its happening by turning away from the fray and pre-occupying ourselves with the pursuit of our own rather small and selfish needs and our own frail quest for safety and security. We are the ones who turned down the volume on the events occurring around us and left the business of government in the hands of this somewhat ragtag gang of elected officials. We are the ones who allowed ourselves to be cowered by the steady bombardment of fear based reporting by both the government and the media. We are the ones who anesthetized ourselves with relatively mindless forms of entertainment and relatively trivial pass times. In short, we turned away from real life by turning material acquisition, entertainment, sports and our virtual life on the web into national pastimes. We did all of this while our national reputation – built so carefully over several hundred years – was badly tarnished, our moral ground abandoned and our habitat and many of the species that reside here poisoned.

Facing Reality

So what do we do now? First and foremost, I believe we need to wake up and admit the reality of our situation. We have some very serious, life and planet threatening problems and neither video games nor our blind worship of the free market economy is going to solve them. Then what? We have to agree – individually and collectively – to start paying attention again. Yes, even if the issues seem overwhelming and we want to run away and hide from them, we need to summon up the courage and the will to re-engage in the governance of our own nation. No matter how awkward we feel, no matter how many mistakes we make, no matter how many outside forces try to convince us that we should leave matters in their hands, we need to reclaim control over our own lives.

For each of us the ways in which we demonstrate this commitment will and should be different. For some of us the place we need to begin will be in our relationships with our children. For others it will be with our significant others or our parents, at our place of work, with friends and colleagues, in the places we worship in the communities in which we live, and with ourselves. Frankly, it does not matter much where each of us begins to retake control over our lives, the only thing that matters is that we do so with as much awareness, consciousness, honesty, immediacy and heart as possible.

Will it be easy? No, it will not! To re-engage in our own lives – especially after this time of denial and withdrawal – we will probably have to deal with some levels of discomfort, give up the safety of our habitual patterns and at least some of the ways in which we currently hide. We will also have to get a little dirty and messy through direct emotional interaction with the people around us. We will have to deal with the effects of our inattention, experience the anger, fear, and confusion of those we have neglected (including our own selves) and eventually we will have to deal with their confusion and despair as well as our own.

Whatever or wherever that next step is, however, the only way that we can once again reclaim our pride and rediscover our sense of meaning and purpose, is to wake up and smell the roses – and the manure – before it is too late. We need to do this as individuals and then collectively as citizens. And we need to do it now, at this very moment in history, at this critical and essential choice point before it is too late. As Marshall McLuhan once said, *"There are no passengers on spaceship Earth, only crew members."*

Chapter Eight
Leading with Wisdom and Diplomacy

—⁓—

"No matter how noble the objectives of a government,
if it blurs decency and kindness, cheapens human life
and breeds ill will and suspicion –
it is an evil government."

— Eric Hoffer

From my perspective, the history of the world can, to a large extent, be viewed as the record of man's attempt to evolve to higher levels of consciousness. It is the record of the journey our species has made from our aquatic beginnings through our animal roots to our experimentation with a host of different strategies – most of them aggressive – in pursuit of meeting our basic requirements for food, water, shelter, clothing and social interactivity. It is, however, also a record of our learning to experience and celebrate life through love, music, art, culture and prayer. Yes, history tells us the story of our journey from early stages of relative unconsciousness to more recent stages in which higher levels of consciousness have become more accessible to all of us.

This story is not, however, a linear one. Humanity, and particularly those of us who are its representatives here in America, have not moved in one continuous flow from one moment to the next accumulating experience and wisdom and then investing these fruits in the next undertaking or period. Instead it appears that humanity has found and lost and lost and found our way again and again in cycles and rhythms that have not always been predictable and, for the most part, have not been the result of conscious choice.

At this moment in history, however, it seems to me that we, the current representatives of this group called humanity, are at a conscious choice point and that a growing number of us are aware of it. Perhaps this is one of the byproducts of our having entered into the Information Age. Perhaps we have finally arrived at that point in our evolution when the right combination of factors is present and we are finally ready to come to a boil.

Fighting the Good Fight

One thing is clear, however, at this moment in our history there is a pitched battle taking place between the forces that want us to take advantage of the lessons of the past and convert them into the foundations for a new period of expanded consciousness and those who are clinging tenaciously to the habits and practices of the past and who firmly believe that the best thing we can do is to keep playing by the same rules that have governed our past – mainly what they call survival of the fittest; between those who look to new forms of intelligent diplomacy and wise and receptive dialogue to resolve our challenges and those who favor the continued use of war and aggression.

While variations on this pitched battle have occurred before, the fact is at earlier times in our history when there were fewer members of our species, a much larger supply of natural resources and significant geographical distances between tribes, this pitched battle between those who wanted to fend for themselves and those who believed in the value of the collective had far less impact on the planet itself and on the other life forms that reside here. Unfortunately, this is no longer true.

300 million plus people in this country alone and about 7 billion people and counting on the planet; rapidly diminishing natural resources; badly polluted air and water; chemically overburdened soil; disappearing species; scientifically engineered food lacking nutritional value; melting ice caps; rising ocean levels; dramatically changing weather patterns, fragile, interdependent economies; instantaneous global communications; and real weapons of mass destruction make it impossible any longer to avoid the consequences of our actions. And these are just a few of the reasons we can no longer allow humanity to meander in cyclical debate between those who advocate survival of the fittest and those who support the path on which collective needs, collaborative efforts and cooperative solutions can be found; between those who favor genuine and compassionate diplomacy and inclusive dialogue and those who look to dominate and disenfranchise.

Indeed, I believe those of us who call ourselves Americans and all others who make up our species around the globe must, for the first time in human history, actually make a conscious choice to utilize wisdom, enlightened leadership and honest dialogue and diplomacy as our primary tools to move us forward. Empty posturing, bullying bravado, isolationism, threats, and acts of war and aggression, and a reliance on survival of the fittest strategies are not just ineffective, they are counterproductive and destructive to our ability to meet our basic needs. Remember Charles Darwin, the Father of Evolution, told us that, *"It is not the strongest or the most intelligent of our species that survive, but the ones most responsive to change."*

This is, of course, not equally obvious to all of the individuals positioned on both sides of the survival of the fittest vs. the collective good equation. Hence the intensity of the struggle that is present in our world today. Unlike some, however, I actually view this intensity with a reasonable degree of optimism because the amount and level of acrimony and divisiveness present today seems to signal that we have left the more superficial periods of this debate behind and are getting to much deeper emotional levels. In short, more and more of those on both sides of this equation sense, even if they do not fully understand, that this is not just another choice point, but perhaps the tipping point and that the actions they take going forward could very well mark an end to one side or another of this debate.

From my perspective, I certainly hope that the momentum finally swings in favor of those of us who understand that on a planet as small, overcrowded and environmentally threatened as this one, there is only one sane choice and that is the rejection of war, aggression and isolationism and the practice of wisdom, enlightened leadership and dialogue and diplomacy.

Moving Beyond War and Aggression

I believe this to be true because even a cursory study of history discloses the fact that war and aggression do not work. While there may be instances when their use has been or may still be necessary to stop the rampages of tyrants or dictators, under the current conditions that exist on this planet one would not only have to be tyrannical and dictatorial, but insane to miss the fact that one cannot drop a nuclear device – no matter how far away – and not end up reaping the impacts locally. One cannot disrupt the flow of essential goods and services in one regional economy without impacting the global economy. One cannot pollute the water, air or soil or reduce the size of forests in one section of the Earth, without impacting the entire planetary ecosystem. Indeed, rational beings can no longer dispute Sir Isaac Newton's contention that *'for every action there is an equal and opposite re-action.'*

So no matter what the color of our skin, no matter what our region, ethnicity, our habits or the scope of our beliefs, it is essential that we remember that beneath our superficial differences we are all members of the same species with the same basic needs and that if we are willing to ensure that all members of our species have enough food, clothing and shelter, and genuine human contact then we can eliminate most of the reasons for war and aggression.

In the meantime, while we are still faced with the terrible repercussions from our past aggression and are still dealing with the regressive and reactive tendencies of others who are still trapped in that paradigm of war and aggression, we should agree to only go to war as a very last resort and then only when our territory and well being are actually threatened or when such action is morally right and supported by solid evidence and the good judgment of our friends and allies.

And if and when we do go to war, we must first take full responsibility for those who we ask to defend us and who, as a result, are placed in harms way. We must agree that if we are forced to defend ourselves we will do so only after adequate planning and with sufficient equipment and enough infrastructure in place to support, protect and nurture our defenders not only while they are away, but when they return and in the long years of healing that follow.

Simultaneous to ensuring this preparedness and while continuing to invest in our defense strategy as a deterrent, we also have to hasten the day when the primary reasons for war and aggression disappear. How do we do this? "Liberty, justice and opportunity for all" is clearly the best place to begin. We can also conduct a more careful and far less biased analysis of history to provide those who rely primarily on facts and reason the opportunity to better understand that the slaughter of over 100,000,000 of our own species during the last century alone clearly did not bring us greater peace, abundance and prosperity or safety and security. It also did not guarantee the survival of any of the tyrants or dictators or the advancement of any of the nations – including our own – who committed acts of war and aggression. And this is only the tale of one century.

Tending to Our Own Wounds

What else can we do? Examine without bias or distortion simulations of the results that continued acts of war and aggression will produce in the future. We certainly have the ability and the computer bandwidth to model these results. In this way even the most ardent supporters of the survival of the fittest school will be forced to recognize that in the end that there is no value to surviving on a planet whose habit and species have been decimated.

What else? Perhaps the most important and most lasting thing each of us can do to advance the cause of genuine peace and harmony on Earth is to do the very challenging, but ultimately necessary individual work of healing our own wounds. To do this we need to have the courage to go into those places inside ourselves where we are holding the residue of physical or emotional abuse, betrayal, abandonment, loss, rejection and other forms of wounding that have shaped both our view and our experience of the world. We need to seek out the assistance of those who can help us to re-experience some of the residual pain that is trapped there, to understand its roots sufficiently to forgive ourselves and others for the roles we and they played, and then we need to release the feelings associated with this wounding so that we can begin to live in the present moment and in full possession of our powers and our wholeness.

Otherwise we are destined to continue living in a world in which far too many of us project and act out our inner wounds on the external landscape and on the other members of our species; a world in which we continue to express disproportionate amounts of judgment, anger and hatred toward those who we call sinful, immoral or different when it is the sin, immorality and the differences within ourselves that we are actually struggling with.

Yes, it is these old personal wounds and not some inherent and pre-ordained flaw or stain on the character of humanity that prompt all of us some of the time and some of us most of the time to act out our wounding and pain on the world around us in the form of individual and collective acts of aggression and war.

So if we will do this very necessary and significant personal work of healing ourselves, our work in the world will get so much easier and the possibilities for genuine peace and harmony will emerge. Does this mean we should immediately melt our swords into plowshares? Probably not! But we can maintain our external vigilance and preparedness while we go about the task of healing our individual and collective wounds and laying the foundation for the remarkable and enlightened future that awaits us on the other side of our pain.

Chapter Nine
Conducting Honest
Public Discourse

—⁓—

"It should never be forgotten by leaders of democratic
nations that nothing except the love and habit of freedom
can maintain advantageous contest with the love
and habit of physical well-being."

— Alexis de Tocquerville

Win at any cost! As we discussed earlier, this seems to be
the new mantra in government, politics, international relations, the corporate arena, sports, schools, churches and community organizations and in far too many of our personal relationships. In fact, this strategy has, especially of late, been on
the rise in each of these areas of our culture to such a degree
that they have, at least in my opinion, now reached epidemic
proportions. Telling lies, giving false testimony, fabricating
evidence, issuing denials and covering up criminal actions,

committing acts of financial malfeasance, leaking inside information, flooding the airways with innuendos and character assassinations, withholding and censoring news, using illegal performance drugs, relying on corporate espionage and bribery, cheating on tests, taxes and others, denying infidelity or sexual preferences and more. And these are only a few of the things that appear to have become not only prevalent in today's public discourse, but equally disturbing, they have become expected and somehow acceptable.

This is not to say that this 'win at any cost' approach has not been used before. Indeed, like the use of the virus of fear and distrust, the history of this planet unfortunately is chock full of examples. What I am saying, however, is that this get-ahead-at-any-cost approach used to be the thing that separated the bad guys from the good guys. Hitler, Stalin, Mussolini, Mao Tse Tung, Pol Pot, Malosevitch, to name just a few in the last century, these were clearly not nice people and their negative and destructive impact on others and on their own nations was almost incalculable.

What has changed, however, is that this approach now seems to characterize the behavior not only of despots, tyrants and the criminal element, but it has become common practice for an increasing number of our political, corporate and religious leaders as well as for us ordinary folks in all segments of our own society. Dangerous? You better believe it! When this strategy is modeled at the highest levels of our government, a little more subtly but just as surely in our highest courts, certainly everywhere in our media, in far too many of our corporate board rooms, churches, in most of our sports stadiums and arenas and even in our class rooms; when this behavior is sanctioned, defended and acted out by our President – we are hanging by a thin branch on the edge of the abyss.

In fact, in my opinion, if we allow this kind of behavior to continue unabated it will, in a relatively short period of time, be as destructive to our way of life as the detonation of a nuclear weapon or the ongoing pollution of our environment for this kind of behavior and the distorted values that underlie them constitute a kind of emotional and spiritual 'dirty bomb' that destroys the fabric of our society.

Am I troubled by this growing wave of what I define as unconscionable and unethical behavior because I am naïve or Puritanical? No, I am troubled by the fact that this behavior, modeled and sanctioned by so many leaders and public figures and practiced by so many of us, has added significantly to the growing level of cynicism and distrust that permeates all levels of our society. It has also done something else, something that for me is equally troubling. It has begun to produce an unprecedented level of indifference and withdrawal from participation by us as citizens not just in governance, but in life in general.

I believe therefore that unless we do something and do this something fast and decisively, we will be in for an even faster decent down a very steep and treacherous slope. Am I exaggerating? I don't think so. I think the same historical record that traces the impact some of the tyrants and despots I named above have had on the world around them, also provides us with indisputable evidence of the path taken by past superpowers and empires during their decline.

Rejecting Quick Fix Answers

So what can we do about this 'win at any cost' mentality and the decline in our values that it demonstrates? As in the other chapters, I do not pretend to have all the answers. In fact, I believe the current expectation by both candidates and voters that those we elect should have all of the answers is one of the primary reasons we are in such enormous difficulty today. The challenges we face are too complex for any one individual or even one political team or party to have all of the answers. Instead what we need is a new form of public debate; an open, intellectually honest public debate that brings the best hearts and minds not only in this country but from around the world together. We need to step back from this time of rigid and mean spirited advocacy and once again invest our curiosity, our ingenuity and our imagination in seeking solutions to the enormous challenges we face.

For my part here are a few more ideas to throw into that pot of this new public discourse. First and foremost, we must be ruthless, immediate, unbiased and relentless in the enforcement of laws and regulations that are currently on the books in both the public and private arenas that prohibit this 'win at any cost' behavior.

In the case of the President or other high elected or appointed officials in any of the three branches of government, as discussed previously, if they lie, mislead, misinform, distort, smear, or violate the rules governing decent, ethical behavior, they should be asked to resign and when there is resistance, they should be impeached or fired, immediately.

This should not be the responsibility of the opposition party or a special prosecutor or a government sub-committee, instead this should be the responsibility of every citizen in this country and, it should be a no brainer! You lie, you cheat, you misinform, you break the rules of decent human interaction – you're gone!

Clearly one of the things we need to do to make this possible is to wake the press up and return it to its rightful place as an independent Fourth Estate. This not only means passing laws to prevent news media from being owned by individuals and organizations whose primary motive is to promote their personal biases and to censor the flow of information, it means journalists, like all other public officials, that lie, distort, misinform, mislead and censor should be run out of their profession. News bureaus that only look at the bottom line and insist on turning news into another form of entertainment should be publicly identified and discredited. Journalism and broadcasting schools should be required to institute higher standards for admission and ensure that comprehensive courses in journalistic ethics are not only required for all students, but are integrated into all course material itself. In short both the organizations and individuals involved in the media should work tirelessly to reclaim their profession before it sinks to even lower levels of the circus side show.

In the corporate arena, executives and leaders should have performance clauses inserted into their contracts that ensure that poor performance as well as unethical behavior of the kind discussed above is more than sufficient cause for immediate dismissal without pay or additional compensation. No golden parachutes, no bonus payments, no stock incentives amounting to millions of dollars for those who fail in this arena. Instead they should be unceremoniously shown the door and, if appropriate, prosecuted in the same way any other individual at lower levels who fails, lies, cheats, distorts, etc. In addition, I believe executives and leaders should operate according to the same code as that of a ship's captain or a military commander. If something happens on their watch, no matter who actually commits the act, then the responsibility lies with the man or woman at the top.

The same should apply to religious leaders. I realize, of course, that this recommendation brings the issue of the separation of church and state even more onto the table. But as we have discussed, it is an essential practice for the well-being of our democracy and so we need to retune the laws encompassing it with great care and consciousness. But abuse of their office by church officials just as abuse by political leaders and executive should be punishable offenses in the public courts.

Follow the same basic principle and you have my prescription for dealing with those who abuse their office and responsibilities in schools, in community organizations, in local businesses, in government agencies, in political and fraternal organizations and in their own personal lives. Unethical, unkind, inhumane, destructive, deceitful behavior should be routed out and eventually, replaced with open, honest discourse and disclosure at all levels of our culture.

Listening to That Inner Voice

Too strict! Impossible to enforce! I don't believe so. If each and every one of us has the courage and discipline to listen to that 'still small inner voice' inside us, the one that knows the difference between what is constructive and what is destructive; between what contributes to the common good and what is simply self-serving, then we can halt this downhill slide rather quickly. And please, don't misunderstand me here. I am not talking about instituting a rigid police state where the ideas, opinions and beliefs of one group or one individual become the rule of the day. I am not talking about imposing arbitrary standards of false morality or sanctimonious ethical standards.   I am not talking about bringing back The Reformation or The Inquisition or ushering in some new version of the Dark Ages – the age we live in is dark enough.

What I am talking about is returning decency, honesty, trust, mutual respect, truth, civility, responsible behavior and genuine, responsible and transparent public discourse to their rightful place at the center of a way of life that is both sane and sustainable.

Chapter Ten
Healing Our Wounds

—ᴿᴿ—

"Whatever the human condition may be, neither an individual nor a nation can ever deliberately commit the least act of injustice without having to pay the penalty for it."

— Henry David Thoreau

If we take our lead, as so many wise beings throughout human history have, from the functioning of the natural world, then it will become clearer to us that attempting to build a structure on unstable soil, in flood planes or washes, or on low tidal areas significantly increases the risk of loosing that structure over time. Following these same natural laws, it is equally true that a physical disturbance to the surface of the Earth or a wound to the flesh of the human body will not heal without appropriate attention and will, if left unattended, leave some degree of permanent dysfunction and scaring.

For those who are students of current events, it should be clear that of late we, in this country, have forgotten a number of these primary lessons that nature teaches us including the two just discussed. As a result we appear to be trying to build the future on the unstable soil of dissension, aggression, lies, deception and disregard for our habitat. We have also forgotten that the wounds we are creating today and those that we have created in the past, whether to the physical body of this planet or to the psyche and spirit of people here in this country and in other nations, will also negatively impact and severely limit our own well being and that of theirs going forward.

I realize, of course, that in this age of terrorism, where many who claim to be our champions constantly scare the pants off us with tales of coming waves of maniacal Jihadists washing over us, my message may seem like a dovish and plaintive plea from a left leaning liberal. I ask you, however, to stay with me a moment and discover if the natural world and our understanding of the dynamics of human interaction do not have some other important lessons for us.

For example, consider what has happened when you have had a physical pain or disturbance in your body – a toothache, a pain in your chest, a stitch in your side, a mole or growth – and not paid attention to it. You get the point! These aches, pains and growths come up when something is out of balance and, if left unattended, they will, most often, increase in frequency and strength until they capture our full attention.

In instances in which we do not attend to these aches or pains, provided they are not signs of a terminal illness, we instead learn to live with them. In these instances the accommodations we make generally involve restructuring some aspect our physical behavior, posture or lifestyle to incorporate the ache or the pain. In fact, we eventually become so accustomed to having the ache or pain in our life that we redefine what we call normal. The limp, the stiffness, the challenge with our bladder, the change in our heart rate or breathing, these signs and signals become normal for us even though they may prevent us from doing things we were accustomed to doing previously with relative ease.

Dealing with Aches and Pains in the Body Politic

If we take these examples and apply them to our political, social, economic and religious/spiritual lives today, I believe, we will find that there are any number of aches and pains that have surfaced over the course of our history and most particularly over the last few decades, that we have not attended to and that have, as a result, become a part of what we now call normal. We've discussed several of these aches and pains already – the fear and distrust that paralyze us, the degradation of our basic values, the undercutting of our democratic process, the acrimony and discord in our public debate, the loss of pride and commitment to excellence in our products and services, and the absence of leadership and vision to name just a few. These social and political aches and pains have caused us to accept conditions and circumstances, here at home and around the world, that just several years ago would have been considered abnormal.

Yes, these discomforts now form the basis of our daily lives, and like the physical aches and pains we discussed earlier, they are forcing us to make accommodations in the present to their presence. These accommodations include more limited lifestyles, more restricted freedoms, a much lower level of confidence in our own government and many of our institutions, much less respect in the world and much greater and more serious threats to our safety, to our democratic process and principles.

If we are content with these accommodations, then clearly we need only continue doing the things we are now doing – avoiding, denying and making more and more accommodations to these aches and pains as they increase.

If, however, we want to lift the restrictions and drop these accommodations and move once again into a new period of national well being, all we have to do is stop doing a number of unhealthy things we are currently doing and begin doing some or all of the positive, constructive and healthy things we know in our hearts we must do.

There is another thing I believe we must do to prevent the American dream from collapsing and that is to deal with the major wounds we are currently inflicting on people in other parts of the world. In considering this, I invite you to once again draw upon your own personal experience as a means of testing the validity of my premise that a wound left unattended will result in some kind of scaring or a limitation in one's range of movement and motion.

Healing Our Current Wounds

The current wounds I am referring to include both the destruction and pollution of the global environment and the subjugation and abuse of other nations. In the case of the environment, as we have already discussed, it is now obvious to all but a few of the most reactionary and greedy among us that unless we change a significant number of our practices the pollution of our air, water, and soil will eventually make this habitat unlivable for the majority of the species who reside here.

In the case of the subjugation and abuse of other people – people of color, people who hold different religious beliefs, people who are less advantaged economically or less advanced technologically – my point may be a little more difficult to grasp at first – especially in this age in which there are constant terror watches at intensities that never drop below the 'serious' level. In fact as a result of the Color Orange announcements and the continual coverage of terror bombings in other countries, far too many of us forget that it is our aggression and our immoral defense of it that have given the Jihadists such fertile ground for the propagation of their absurd brand of religious malevolence. But before some of you turn away because you do not agree with my assessment of the political motives of those on either side, I ask you to again use your own life experience as a reference.

Consider for a moment the subject of guilt. Please call to mind something you feel guilty about. It could be a small something you did yesterday or the day before – a small lie you told, an error of intentional omission, or a relatively minor error you made and did not admit or a commitment you made to do or go somewhere that you did not keep – or it may be a much larger something you did months or years ago – an infidelity, betrayal, an act of physical or emotional abuse or what you define as cowardice.

I will bet if you allow yourself to dig around for just a few seconds you will find yourself remembering something you did – the betrayal in a friendship, the lie you told, the injury you caused, the something you stole or cheated on, the something you denied or turned away from. And I'll bet if you allow yourself to admit it you will find that when you feel the feelings associated with this particular memory, you still feel some of the same intensity of feeling today that you did months or years ago when you first committed the action.

You see guilt, left unattended, continues to exist in much the same way as the wounds to the Earth and to our bodies left untreated also continue. And these psychic/emotional wounds also leave scars that are just as limiting and danger-ous to our well being as the physical ones. In fact, in many instances, these psychic wounds are even more debilitating because although we are constantly dealing with their impact, these scars are not as visible or accessible to us as those left by physical action. This lack of visibility then allows us to avoid and deny them. *"Not me! I haven't done anything wrong. There is nothing I feel guilty about, nothing that I regret."* And yet even a casual encounter with the memory of one of our past actions, if we are honest with ourselves, causes us to re-experience much of the guilt of the original action or event.

What's my point? That our current actions that pollute the Earth or that injure people in other parts of the world con-tribute to the accumulation of significant amounts of both individual and collective guilt. And this guilt, in turn, con-tributes to the loss of our self-respect, lower levels of pas-sion and energy, increased amounts of confusion and decreased levels of self-confidence, to name just a few. And over time, these factors cause other things – our withdrawal from circumstances in which our actions could be discovered or in which they could occur again, sometimes they prompt excessively aggressive behavior that masks our original actions. At other times the price we pay is a kind of depression, individual and collective, that grows insidiously in intensity.

Dealing with the Wounds of the Past

For me there are a number of other psychic and spiritual wounds that we carry – individually and collectively – that today are contributing to our loss of self-respect, self-confidence, our reduced energy and our diminishing sense of passion and purpose as a nation. Among these are the scars that have resulted from the subjugation we, as invaders and colonizers, visited upon the indigenous people who were here when we arrived; from the enslavement of our black and brown brothers and sisters who were brought here against their will; from acts of aggression and violence acted out by both sides in the civil war that continue to separate North from South; from the bigotry and prejudice practiced by various religious sects against other religious sects; and from the aggressiveness and bias demonstrated by historic immigrant minorities toward more recent arrivals. Additional psychic wounds also come from the abuse visited by men on women over centuries and from the terrible crimes adults have and continue to visit upon children. And these are only some of the psychic wounds we have inflicted that continue to hold us hostage and continue to release their toxicity – consciously and unconsciously – into the hearts and minds of people throughout this nation. And they will continue to do so and in the process limit us and contribute to our downhill slide as a nation unless we do something about them.

How do we deal with these old psychic wounds – some of which were inflicted originally by our parents or their parents or grandparents? I believe that once again simple solutions are better and much more effective. I also believe that solutions that focus our attention first on our individual responsibility are most necessary and essential for unless and until we learn to be responsible for ourselves, we cannot hope to lead others.

So we need to start with awareness and admit within our hearts what we – or those who have come before us – have done. We must then allow ourselves to feel the sadness and pain these actions have caused others.

The next thing we need to do is to admit our crimes and misdemeanors out loud and without any attempt to deny, justify or rationalize them. The third thing we must do is to apologize openly and transparently to the individuals against whom we – or our forefathers – have committed these crimes or to their heirs if they are no longer alive. Finally, we must be willing to feel deeply enough into our sadness and pain to ensure that we will not commit similar acts in the future and we must make this commitment loud enough for the entire world to hear.

Do we pay reparations or make other financial gestures? We can, but frankly, I do not believe financial reparations will solve anything. The reparations will be paid by the heirs of the perpetrators to the heirs of the victims and, in the end it is not reparations but genuine, heartfelt apologies that will do the most good.

Other things I would recommend. We must examine our laws and policies to be certain that they do not contain the seeds of future abuses. I also recommend we take a close and careful look at our educational system and at our educators themselves to be certain that we identify and root out all levels of bias, bigotry and ignorance that contributed to these atrocities in the past. We should also make every effort to re-write our history books to report these past atrocities and the lessons we have learned from them accurately. Only in this way will future generations have the opportunity to learn from our errors and avoid similar mistakes.

I also recommend that we remain constantly vigilant in regard to our own actions that stem from the biases, prejudices and the habituated negative responses we have learned from others. I recommend that we do not hold ourselves to such impossibly high standards of perfection that when we slip or fall back into old patterns we declare ourselves broken and use this as a reason for returning to our negative patterns. Instead I recommend that when we commit acts that are selfish, hurtful and destructive toward others we forgive ourselves, ask the forgiveness of those we have injured and then get on with the business of finding more positive and collaborative ways of living life in accordance with our basic values and principles.

And finally, I recommend that as soon as possible, we begin altering our behavior in regard to people around the world to whom we are currently doing harm. As soon as possible we must do our best to work with them to repair the damage we have caused and also turn our attention to repairing the damage to the Earth and to the other species that reside here.

In this way, and only in this way, can we move beyond both the physical and psychic wounds and the limitations and burdens they represent and begin to retake some of the moral high ground we have squandered so badly over the course of our history and especially these last six years. Only in this way can we eliminate the psychic burden we carry and thereby rekindle the promise of the land of the free and the home of the brave where those who seek refuge from oppression and from limitation are welcomed and allowed, through their own sweat and talent, to seek the promise of new opportunity.

Chapter Eleven
Retaking the High Ground

—ᛩᛩ—

"The power of a man
is his present means
to obtain some future good."

— Thomas Hobbes

We will certainly take more than a few major strides forward in reclaiming the high ground if we have the courage to heal the wounds of the past, but there are a number of other things I believe we must also do. Here in this present moment we must align our actions with our values and thereby model for ourselves, our children and for others around the world, the kind of behaviors that contribute to a genuinely sane and sustainable democratic world.

In order to accomplish this alignment we must stop all of the empty posturing, the misleading rhetoric and the holier than thou flaunting of our so called Christian values that have characterized so much of our behavior of late and instead we must start demonstrating the kind of genuine compassionate and enlightened behavior that will allow us once again to speak as champions of the democratic process.

Unfortunately, so many of our actions over the last several decades have undercut that right, but none as blatant as our fabrication of evidence to justify our second invasion of Iraq. Yes, our indefensible invasion of another sovereign nation, a country that posed no direct danger to us, changed the rules by which civilized nations in the modern age deal with each other.

Preceding the invasion another unconscionable event occurred – the election of George W. Bush as President of the United States by the U.S. Supreme Court. Taken together, these two events not only knocked us off our pedestal as the world's largest, most prosperous and most magnanimous democracy, they also took away our right and privilege to hold any other nation on the face of the Earth accountable for their acts against their people or against humanity as a whole.

So what specifically can we do to reclaim the moral high ground? And perhaps of equal import, what do we want to do? I offer these thoughts and recommendations for your consideration, but I also remind you that the most viable and valuable answers to these questions must be discovered in open, honest public discourse that includes the participation of a number of essential and conscious stakeholders.

Admitting Our Mis-steps

From my perspective, asking the question about Iraq – not from a partisan political standpoint, but rather as mature and discerning citizens committed to our well-being – will allow us to not only better understand what occurred that caused us to misstep so badly, but what we need to do to avoid this kind of failure in the future. I also believe an open and honest examination of the actions we took on the road to the illegal invasion of Iraq will require that we make some significant changes in our political process, certainly our definition of what constitutes ethical journalism and reporting, the role of our leaders and the responsibilities each of us as citizens have in our governance.

In examining the path we took I believe we will be forced to admit that we cannot continue to delegate our sovereignty so completely to our elected representatives while we go about demonstrating the kind of somnambulistic, head down behavior that characterizes so much of our contemporary lives today. I believe we can accurately conclude that if we do this we cannot expect a democracy to survive.

Instead, we are going to have to drag this issue out into the open air – not in some acrimonious conservative against liberal debate, or biased political dialogue – but as a highly moral, civil and ethical conversation in which we, as citizens of this democracy, examine our own culpability as well as that of our leaders. Yes, unless we acknowledge our mistakes and do all that we can to rectify them, we are setting ourselves up for a lot of the long term pain and suffering, the same kind of pain and suffering we just discussed that has plagued us as a result of our treatment of the indigenous people and our black brothers and sisters. If we need further justification for considering this, we need only reconsider one of Newton's Laws that states that *'for every action there is an opposite and equal reaction.'*

We would also be wise to redirect our attention to the guidance of two remarkable individuals, Dwight D. Eisenhower who warmed us so eloquently during his farewell address of the dangers of the military-industrial complex, and General Maxwell Taylor another highly decorated veteran who, in his critique of our involvement in Vietnam said, *"We didn't know ourselves... we didn't know our South Vietnamese allies... and we knew even less about North Vietnam. So until we know the enemy, our allies and ourselves, we'd better keep out of this dirty kind of business. It's very dangerous!"* Sound familiar?

In seeking an answer to the second question about the election of George W. Bush by a philosophically biased U.S. Supreme Court, I believe we will have the opportunity to redefine the concepts of rank and privilege in this country, and in doing so, perhaps allow the next stage of democracy to begin.

Yes, I believe an examination of this second question holds enormous riches for if we go deeply enough into it, we may discover sufficient motivation to take the leap that until now we have avoided – the leap of recognizing that democracy is a valuable evolutionary step for all nations on this earth.

First and foremost, as I said previously, this examination will allow us to redefine the process by which we nominate and appoint our justices. This may mean that we restructure the process and require the election of all judges, limit their terms – especially on all high courts – or find other sane means to restore integrity and balance to our judicial system. The second thing this examination of the intrusion of our courts into the process of electing a president will do is prompt us to stop inflating our sense of self importance and to stop lording over the rest of humanity as the sole keepers of the truth. Instead if we admit our frailties, offer our experience and shine the spotlight of attention on the value of democracy itself, the next stages of its evolution as a way of achieving more enlightened government for the planet can begin.

Yes, by admitting that we are only the temporary guardians – and flawed and imperfect guardians at that – of this process called democracy – we can allow others around the world to understand that democracy does not belong to America, but instead that it was only birthed or more accurately re-birthed here in relatively recent times. We can allow them to understand that democracy also belongs to them and to future generations as well and that it should not and cannot be limited by the way we demonstrate or practice it.

So if we are willing to examine how the distortion and abuse of own electoral process during the election of George W. Bush to a first term by the courts led us astray and how we abused our own system of government in our second invasion of Iraq, perhaps we can allow democracy to grow and mutate naturally across the face of this planet, not as our gift, but rather as a next iteration of a form of government that can lead all of us to a higher evolution of human consciousness.

Indeed, just as the written language, the use of colored symbols and signs, the development of tribal councils, the invention of the printing press, and hundreds of thousands of other steps on the road to higher human consciousness were birthed in various place around the globe, so democracy came into being here in recent history to be shared with everyone as the foundation for a new age of participation and cooperation, a new age of individual empowerment in which all human beings are treated equally and we recognize the 'unalienable Rights' of all and 'that among these are Life, Liberty and the pursuit of Happiness.'

Chapter Twelve
Finding Genuine Solutions

—ɯ—

"Don't be afraid to take a big step
if one is indicated.
You can't cross a chasm
in two small jumps."

— David Lloyd George

When asked to do something or to go somewhere, I often hear people say, 'I'll try to do that' or 'I'll try to be there.' Funny thing about trying, along time ago I learned a very valuable lesson – there is no such thing as trying. One cannot try to do anything or try to go anywhere. One is either in some stage of doing a thing or going to a place or one is some stage of not doing a thing or not going to a place.

I realize, of course, you may think that I'm just splitting verbal hairs here. But that is not the case at all. And I believe if you take a few moments to verify my claim against your own life experience you will agree that there is something here worth talking about in much greater detail, something that relates directly to many of the challenge we face today as a nation.

For example, when you tell someone you will 'try to do something' or that you will 'try to meet them at an appointed time and place,' what are your really saying? Are you saying you will do the thing or actually show up at the appointed place or are you using the verb 'try' to give yourself an alternative or a way out in case you do not or cannot do the thing or get to the place at the appointed time?

What does your experience tell you? My life experience tells me the latter is true. When I use the verb 'try' I am not fully committed to doing the thing or showing up at the appointed place. And commitment is, after all, what generally differentiates success from failure.

W. H. Murray, who led one of the earliest Scottish expeditions to climb Mount Everest, had this to say about commitment:

> *"Until one is committed there is*
> *hesitancy, the chance to draw back.*
> *Concerning all acts of initiative and*
> *creation there is one elementary rule –*
> *the ignorance of which kills countless*
> *ideas and splendid plans.*
> *That moment when one definitely*
> *commits oneself, then Providence moves too.*
> *all sorts of things occur to help one that*
> *would otherwise never have occurred."*

I am making this point here and now because as I continue to invite you to turn your attention to the search for genuine solutions to the major challenges our nation faces today, I want you to consider how many people in public office and in positions of leadership tell us they are going to 'try' to solve this problem or 'try' to fix that difficulty.

Eliminating Those Tired Old Excuses

The truth, of course, is that most people in public office, just like most of us in our personal lives, use 'trying' as a way of avoiding actually making a commitment to solve the challenges – both small and large – that we face. These public office holders, like many of us, talk a great deal about possible solutions. They form study groups and committees to consider the topics. They seek compromises and accommodations around them. They even make public pronouncements and campaign promises about what they will do about these challenges once they are elected. But by and large what they do not do is to actually commit – in the way that W. H. Murray describes it – to do whatever it takes, for as long as it takes no matter what sacrifices are required or changes in their own behaviors and beliefs or ours are necessary to solve these problems and fix these difficulties.

No, most people in public positions, and this includes all of our elected officials some of the time and some of them all of the time, realize that making these kinds of commitments will probably cost them points with some segment of their constituency in the latest public opinion surveys, lose them contributions from some of their corporate donors, or worse yet, require an unflinching level of focus and energy, perhaps all of their focus and energy.

So, most office holders and candidates, just like many of us, soon discover that if they insert the word 'try' into their pronouncements to a public accustomed to accepting 'trying' over 'doing,' they can always throw their hands up, point the finger at someone else and say 'I tried.' And we, the people, like lemmings, will let them sail off into the sunset to play golf or make a boodle of money on speaking tours while we turn our attention to the next sycophant who pops up on the horizon with new tales of the things they are going to 'try' to do for us.

This is as true today as it was during Winston Churchill's time when he had this to say about leaders who ignored Hitler. *"They go on in strange paradox, decided only to be undecided, resolved to be irresolute, adamant for drift, solid for fluidity, all powerful to be impotent."*

Yes, as a nation we have become accustomed to our leaders doing a hell of lot of 'trying' and not very much doing. And we, the people, who they purport to serve, have become accustomed to all of their public blathering and blubbering and to settling for minimal solutions to problems and difficulties that are weighing us down, destroying the promise of this great nation and even placing the very planet in serious jeopardy. We, the proud, the brave and the free, have become accustomed to being grateful for the mediocre, the insufficient and the inadequate trying. Talk about fiddling while Rome burns!

So how do we move beyond this ineffective and self-defeating state of affairs? I suggest we begin by eliminating 'trying' as an acceptable word from our cultural dictionary. We can do it first, in all areas of our individual lives and, second, as quickly as possible, we can eliminate this word from the national dialogue as well. For I have said before, the real power to change the course of this nation always begins with each of us as individuals and with our courage and willingness to change our own behavior. The more we shift our behavior from destructive to constructive, the more it is possible to shift the behavior of this nation and eventually this world.

I realize, of course, that relative to the massive challenges we face – environmental catastrophes, war, pestilence and disease, terrorism, etc. – the elimination of the verb 'to try' from our personal and public vocabulary may seem like a pretty puny solution, but I challenge you. For just a week or two experiment with eliminating it from your vocabulary, stop using it as a way out of commitment and see what happens!

Holding Our Leaders Accountable

What else can we do? Start holding those who lead us – at work, in our churches, in our schools, in our communities and in our state and national governments – accountable for finding solutions to real and eminent problems and difficulties that we face. If they cannot or will not make a commitment to do so, we should invite them to find other professions. If someone slips past us and gets into office before we discover they cannot or will not make this commitment to do whatever it takes to find genuine and constructive solutions to the problems we face, then we should hold them accountable by impeaching them or voting to send them packing as soon as possible.

Unfortunately, however, in a world that is moving at warp speed, the average term of office for most elected officials is too long to depend on this device alone. So we must learn to raise our voices much more quickly. We must learn to lift our heads from the daily push and pull in our own lives as soon as we see that someone is 'trying' and 'talking' rather than 'committing' and 'acting.' We must raise our voices so that those in public office will know we are not going to stand for it. You see, we too have to stop 'trying' and start 'committing' to responsible self-governance.

If necessary we have to be committed enough to this path to take the time to go to their offices and speak personally to our elected officials. Where this is not possible we have to call them, write them letters and emails, circulate partitions, join demonstrations and, as I said before, if necessary, participate in general strikes to get their full attention.

Launching A Tax Revolt

We also have to remember that the money that pays their salaries, buys their healthcare coverage, allows them to travel and run for office and the money they commit to various bills and policy decisions is our money. So if they will not listen in any other way, we have to stop making the political contributions and stop paying taxes. For in the end, without money they can only sit around absently twiddling their thumbs.

"It's against the law not to pay taxes," you say!   Perhaps! Although there are some who have demonstrated that there is a significant difference between the responsible withholding of taxes and the attempt to avoid them. I am not suggesting that you refuse to pay your taxes and then use the money to buy a new flat screen television or to renovate your kitchen. No, I am suggesting that you take the money you are scheduled to use to pay your taxes and put it into an escrow account and then tell the IRS and your elected officials that you will pay your taxes when they remember they work for you and not for themselves and, most especially, when they stop 'trying' and start 'doing' something about the problems and difficulties that need immediate attention.

And when they tell you it is un-American not to pay your taxes; when they tell you that 'trying' is part of the American way; when they tell you that all of the public blabbering and blubbering and finger pointing and name calling and pork barreling is unavoidable, you simply have to remind them that our forefathers fought the American Revolution not just to end oppression, but to end unfair taxation as well. You only have to remind them to read The Declaration of Independence and remember our forefathers believed that:

"Governments are instituted among Men, deriving their just powers from the consent of the governed, – That whenever any Form of Government becomes destructive of these ends, it is the Right of the People to alter or to abolish it, and to institute new Government, laying its foundation on such principles and organizing its powers in such form, as to them shall seem most likely to effect their Safety and Happiness."

Chapter Thirteen
Moving Beyond Scarcity

—ɯ—

"I sit on a man's back, choking him
and making him carry me, and yet assure
myself and others that I am very sorry
for him and wish to lighten his load by
all possible means – except getting off his back."

— Leo Tolstoi

The virus of fear and distrust that permeates the atmosphere in this country today is, as we have previously talked about, not new. This disease has haunted humanity from its earliest days and certainly from the time when power within various cults and later within a number of organized clans and religions was transferred from the patriarchs and matriarchs who founded them into the hands of followers who unfortunately, lacking the capacity, vision and authenticity of the founders, resorted to other means to keep the faithful in line. Yes, these less gifted souls who followed the founders often found it necessary to utilize fear and superstition to keep the faithful motivated. Do this and you will be punished! Do that and you will be saved! Go against this pronouncement and you are evil and will be caste out. Do what we tell you to do and you are good! Suppress your curiosity, deny your innate intelligence, contradict your inner wisdom, rely on us as your intermediaries in your relationship with the Divine and you will be given a place in Heaven or Nirvana. Follow your curiosity or the guidance of the feminine (inner or outer) and take a bite of the apple of The Tree of Knowledge and you will forever be stained.

I know that I am on tender ground here. For in our country today it is okay, in fact, it is fair game to point out flaws in our political, corporate and judicial systems and in the leaders within these areas. It is also perfectly acceptable to suggest that they utilize fear and distrust as a means of keeping us confused and dispirited and themselves in positions of power. However, unless the leader of a church or a religious sect wanders off the path into embezzlement or, heaven forbid, gay sex, to suggest that they or other members of their ministries utilize fear and distrust as the means of keeping the faithful in line gets a little dicey.

If, however, we are to actually clear the air and finally discover a true antidote to this deadly virus that infects our culture, I believe we must identify and root out its use in all areas of our culture – and religion is certainly one of them. In saying this, however, I want to be clear that I believe in God, Spirit, the Divine, or whatever other names the omnipotent and omniscient, central, organizing source of all life is known by. What I do not believe in, however, is the omnipotence and omniscience of man. Nor do I believe that for the most part those who claim to represent the Divine are actually able to accurately interpret the teachings of the original founders of their religions – Jesus Christ, Buddha, Zoroaster, Krishna, Mohammed, Moses, etc. In fact, to the contrary, I believe that many of these religious managers – throughout the course of history – have, in the absence of the real and original power held by the founders, succumbed to the use of a number of deceptive and destructive means to keep themselves in power.

Curing the Virus of Scarcity

One of these deceptive and destructive means is the virus of scarcity. Of course, religions are not alone in using it. Many of the bureaucrats who occupy positions of leadership in our own and other governments, much like the followers who come after the original religious leaders, often fail to measure up in vision, capacity and moral authority to the founders. As a result, they too resort to the use of the virus of scarcity to keep us numbly walking along the path of dumb compliance.

Of course, like fear and distrust, scarcity is, for the most part, also an illusion. And by this I do not mean to imply that there is never a cause for fear or distrust or that there are never conditions under which scarcity exists. What I am saying is that conditions under which fear, distrust and scarcity are found are far less frequent as natural occurrences than some would have us believe. In fact, times of actual danger when the biologically encoded fight or flight mechanism kicks in are almost miniscule in the life of the average American. Whereas the number of times when emotional fear and distrust are triggered by external influences and internally held beliefs are substantial.

The same is true for scarcity. Unlike people who reside in other lands where poor quality soil and the lack of potable water makes scarcity a real issue, the majority of Americans are blessed with lives in which genuine scarcity is not that prevalent. Again, this is not to say that there are not far too many people in this country who live below the poverty line and who suffer from the effects of insufficient food, water, shelter and clothing. But for these souls there have been, at least until relatively recently, some government programs and a number of local church and community outreach efforts that provide some degree of support. This does not, of course, lessen the difficult conditions under which these fellow human beings who are homeless and poor live nor does it make their situation in any way acceptable. I only make this point to differentiate these disenfranchised Americans from their counterparts in other places around the world where no support services whatsoever exist.

Eliminating the Illusion of Scarcity

My primary contention here is, however, that the virus of scarcity, like those of fear and distrust, while sometimes the result of real conditions and circumstances such as natural catastrophes, untillable or uninhabitable land, and of course, the man made crises of war and pillage, are for the most part and for most Americans emotionally triggered experiences that result from distorted and artificial beliefs propagated by our government and our religious and economic institutions. They are also, of course, perpetuated by our educational institutions and, in the modern age spread rapidly by the media.

Yes, the virus of scarcity, like that of fear and distrust, comes into play most of the time as a result of the limited beliefs and the systems we human beings have created. And one of the most dominant of these beliefs is that which holds that it is justifiable to control the availability and distribution of natural resources.

For the sake of this discussion, I will limit the scope of this discussion to challenges we face here in our nation and I will use hunger as my example. Clearly there are a lot of Americans who experience varying degrees of hunger each day. Indeed, there are more than 60 million Americans – about one in five of us – who subsist near to or below what is called 'the poverty line.' This number includes children, adults and seniors of all races and creeds who do not have the means, skills, emotional and psychological balance, physical capacities, energies or sometimes the circumstances or the desire required to earn enough money to pay for some or all of their daily needs.

At the same time, there are many millions of Americans who do have the means, skills, emotional and psychological balance, energies and the desire required to earn enough money to pay for their daily needs. As a result we define the conditions under which the first group exists as scarcity and the conditions under which the second group exists as normal to abundant.

If, however, we remove the artificial influences created by the concept of private ownership of natural resources and by the controlled and manipulated distribution of goods that are present in the free market economy and look instead at the aggregate amount of natural resources available and the goods that are produced and distributed as byproducts of them in the United States, I believe you will reach the same conclusion I have. There is more than enough food, water, shelter, and clothing available to care not just for some of our people some of the time, but to provide amply for all of our people all of the time.

Debunking the Free Market Economy

I realize that earlier when I said that a number of religions continue to control the faithful through the propagation of fear and distrust, I stepped across a line. I am now crossing another line that protects what is perhaps our other most sacrosanct institution, our free market economy, from any criticism about its perfection. But cross this line I will for I believe that unless we alter our tenacious clinging to our current worship of a free market economy we will never be successful in laying the foundation for a sane and sustainable future. Indeed, in order to truly rediscover the path toward fulfilling the American Promise, I believe we must revisit our blind attachment to our current economic system. For inherent in the promise of democracy is the fact that people are – *'endowed by their creator with certain unalienable rights – that among these are life, liberty and the pursuit of Happiness.'*

Notice that democracy as it was established here in America by our forefathers spoke of rights that were 'unalienable' and 'endowed by our creator.' They also spoke of *'all human beings treated equally and with freedom of opportunity and justice for all.'* Our forefathers did not suggest that 'all' included only Republicans or Democrats. Only white folks or those who were educated. They did not say that some human beings should be confined to poverty and hunger and that others should through cunning, stealth, criminal action, luck, talent, good fortune or some combination of these factors have the right to opportunities far greater than others and to have access and control over natural resources and goods that are necessary for adequate survival and well-being of everyone.

No, our forefathers were rather clear in their articulation of the principles upon which they were founding this democracy. As a result, I believe that if we value democracy; if we believe in the spirit and intent on which this nation was founded, then we must also believe that the natural resources that are part of this nation and the goods that are produced from them belong not just to a few of our citizens, but to all of our citizens regardless of race, creed, or color. For in my experience I never met a person who claimed to have created the natural resources that some of us so willingly claim as our personal property. No, we did not create the earth, the water and the air that sustains us. It is only through the perpetuation of a distorted and short term view of the law of survival of the fittest (or the most cunning or the most aggressive or the luckiest or the most criminal) that some among us have taken possession of these God created and God given resources.

Exploring the Limits of Personal Wealth

So I believe that if we are ever to become a truly democratic society we must revisit the right to own personal property and to accumulate personal wealth, not with an eye to
eliminating these rights – for I believe they offer positive
benefits by fostering healthy competition – but certainly
with an eye to modifying them so that these individual rights
do not work to the detriment of the common and greater
good. In other words, when the rights of some to accumulate personal wealth prevent others from being able to meet
their basic needs for food, water, shelter, clothing and social
interaction, then I believe we must look to adjust our beliefs
about these rights and find intelligent, mature, sane and sustainable ways to regulate them with much greater awareness
and consciousness. This, I believe, is the true promise of
democracy.

And if we can ever get to this place where we are capable of
demonstrating this as truth within our own borders, and if
we are ever capable of arriving at the conclusion that
democracy is the next step not just for those of us who call
ourselves American citizens, but for the citizens of the planet as a whole, then it will also be true that this same kind of
restructuring of the free market economy will need to be
accomplished on a global basis. For in the end, when each
citizen of this nation, and eventually, each member of our
global community finally admits that none of us are free
until all of us are free; and none of us is safe or secure until
all of us have enough food, water, shelter, clothing and
social interaction, will we truly be moving toward a time of
peace on Earth. Yes, individually and collectively we must

move beyond the viruses of scarcity, fear and distrust and step fully into the zone of abundance and gratitude for in this way and only in this way we will stop sacrificing the well-being of the many for the benefit of the few; only in this way will we finally get to some of the true root causes of aggression, terrorism and war and eliminate them.

Chapter Fourteen
Turning Out the Money Lenders

—⁓—

"The superior man seeks
what is right,
the inferior man
what is profitable."

— Confucius

Most of us are familiar with the biblical story about Christ chasing the money lenders out of the temple. For my part, I am not sure when or where I first heard it. Most likely it was in Sunday School, although it is also possible that I learned about it from one of those early C.B. DeMille biblical spectaculars that traditionally resurface around Easter each year. No matter where or how I first learned about it, however, what was true for me at the time and is still true for me today is that I am not sure if Christ wanted the money lenders out of the temple or out of society as a whole.

It has always been an intriguing question for me and I

believe for many others – and that includes anyone who has ever paid interest on anything from a credit card purchase to a home, automobile, personal or business loan. Indeed, anyone who has ever interfaced with a money lender – those who today are more politely called bankers and investment specialists – has probably wondered what the world would be like without the presence of this profession which, along with those who share their sexual favors with strangers, is said to be one of the oldest professions in the world. In fact, as long as one man has by talent, cunning, criminal act, hard work, inheritance, pure luck or some combination of these factors had more of something than another, this practice of exchanging his surplus for repayment of the amount (principle) plus some additional sum (interest) has been said to make the world go around.

Of course, none of us will ever know for certain whether Christ was opposed to this profession in general, or if he simply wanted there to be a clear distinction between God's business and man's. Of late, however, I have begun to hold out hope that he was inclined toward the first of these choices. Why? Because as I look around me in the world today I cannot imagine a scenario that would not be improved and, in many cases dramatically so, by significantly reducing the presence and influence of the money lenders and the money manipulators.

I know this is pretty heretical stuff especially in this land of free enterprise where economics is next to godliness and my continuing pursuit of this line of reasoning may well disqualify me from ever receiving a loan of any kind for any purpose ever again. But since I did not flinch in pointing out the frailties of organized religion, government or business in spreading the viruses of fear, distrust and scarcity; and since I did not hesitate to suggest that we should revisit the subject of private ownership in a mature and intelligent way, not necessarily eliminating it, but weighing it against the right of the common good, I will not finch from dealing with the subject of usury and money manipulation either.

Putting A Cap On

Even the briefest incursion into this forbidden zone leads me to conclude that most of humanity would be far better off it we declared an end to usury – especially at the level of greed in which it is currently practiced. Or if not an end to usury, at the very least, the placing of very real, immediate and significant limits on the amount of interest whether it is paid in beads, cows, sex, or dollars that a lender can charge a borrower.

"Foolishness," you say! *"The world would come to a screeching halt."* *"I mean, who would provide the capital for business growth?"* *"Who would allow Tom Smith to get the money he needs to open his shop, pay for his child's education or buy that house his wife wants?"* *"What would happen to mutual funds and CEO stock options?"* *"Who would finance all of this if usury was eliminated or significantly reduced?"* *"What are you Cappannelli – some kind of an anarchist or socialist or communist?"*

No, I am none of the above, but that does not prevent me from recommending that we take a very hard and careful look at the way we are doing things – especially around capital exchange. Would the world come to a screeching halt if usury was eliminated or significantly reduced? No, but the world would certainly change, that much is certain, and especially for most of humanity as well as for the rather sizable army of individuals who make their living studying the ebb and flow of money, manipulating its availability and making a living as money lenders!   But the world will not, in my opinion, either implode or explode without this profession.

What would happen is that most of the hot air and a lot of the excessive fat and greed would be taken out of the system and therefore those who by talent, cunning, criminal acts, hard work, inheritance, luck or some combination of these factors who have accumulated more than they need would have to make do with less and find some other way to make a living. And, of course, the greatest change, and the one really worth dwelling on, is that most of us who make up humanity would no longer have to spend the majority of our lives in literal servitude to the false god of debt.

Worshipping the God of Debt

Why do I call debt 'a false god?'   For me it is pretty clear. Let us say my wife wants me to purchase a house just like the one Tom Smith's wife wants him to buy, a nice house in an average American neighborhood in an average American city for a relatively average American price. And let us say the sale price is $250,000. Since I don't have the $250,000 sitting around in a shoe box under my bed and I no longer live in a world where I, as the purchaser, can go to the owner and make my own arrangements for the payment of the $250,000 over a time period mutually agreeable to both, I now go to a middleman – my banker – and apply for a loan. Depending on my credit scores, my demonstrated income level and other factors that are evaluated by the bank as well as the amount of money the middleman wants to make on the transaction, I am required to come up with between 10% and 20% of the loan amount in cash in the form of a deposit. The final loan amount also, of course, includes points (the amount of money I pay the bank for making the loan) insurance costs, other bank fees, fees paid to a mortgage broker (another middleman) who arranges the loan with the bank and other closing costs.

Since most home loans involve a thirty year repayment plan, let's use this as the model for my loan. So my loan amount is approximately $230,000 plus closing costs and my interest payment – picking another average – let us say it is 7% over 30 years.

Now because I am an average American, I pay my loan payments on time most of the time, but I do not have the ability to pay additional amounts each month that would allow me to reduce my principle sooner while paying off my interest. As a result let us say it takes me the full 30 years to pay off the loan. Using all of the calculations listed above, the amount of interest I pay over this 30 year period is approximately $525,000. Yes, that's right! Even though the original selling price of my home was only $250,000, by the time I am finished paying the loan off I end up paying my bank or lending institution approximately $525,000 in interest.

This amount does not, of course, include the profit the middleman, my mortgage broker, makes, or the amount my bank makes on the money I am required to keep in a checking or saving account in his bank during the period of my loan, nor does it include the profit the bank also makes on the money (principle and interest) that I repay to the bank on my original loan amount over the course of the thirty years that the bank lends to other people at similar or often times higher rates of interest.

Now to be fair I have to admit that there are costs associated with the handling of my loan by the bank so those need to be factored in, but somehow I have a very hard time believing that it costs my bank anywhere near $525,000 to process my monthly check for the payment of my principle and interest. But let us give my bank the benefit of the doubt times four or five. Let's say it costs my bank $50,000 over the term of my loan to administer it. Then let us even add in some amount for the risk my bank takes in giving me the loan in the first place. Of course, that risk is substantially lessened by the fact that to qualify for my loan in the first place I had to fill out enough application forms to provide the bank with more information about me than I myself possess. Then, of course, there is the ultimate risk mitigator – the bank and not me that owns the deed to the house I have just purchased and if I default on the loan the bank gets to sell the house on the open market for whatever increase in value the house has accumulated between the time of my purchase and the time of my default on the loan.

You get the point! Money changing (lending) is a pretty terrific business! It is also an incredibly profitable business even when it is conducted out in the open with some semblance of scrutiny (the amount and level of scrutiny, of course, depends on whether a conservative or liberal administration is in office). And it is obscenely profitable when it is conducted by what are traditionally referred to as unethical lenders. Although when one considers the recent sub-prime mortgage melt-down and many of the other questionable and shady credit card and bank debit card practices with compounding rates and hidden charges practiced in the industry, one wonders if there really is a difference between so called ethical and unethical lenders.

To further substantiate this point one only has to consider the fact that at no time during this most recent sub-prime meltdown did any of the lending institutions who were directly responsible for granting loans to unqualified and uniformed loan applicants in the first place offer to freeze their APR rates. This one simple act could have averted the entire crisis, but of course it would also have reduced the amount of profit made by the banks.

Adding Up the Numbers

So let's take a final look at this transaction from my side as a borrower. Over the course of thirty years my house (which the bank owns until my final payment is processed) that I originally purchased for $250,000 actually costs me approximately $775,000 in principle and interest plus taxes and the cost of repairs, maintenance and improvement. For the sake of argument, let's estimate (on the conservative side) that over the period of time I have lived in the house it has cost me an average of $5000 a year in repairs, maintenance and improvements. That means that I have spent an additional $150,000 on these costs over the life of my loan.

At the same time, of course, if I purchased my home in a

reasonably stable neighborhood, my home has increased in value over this same period and at the time I pay it off, traditionally a time when I am ready to retire and downsize, the value of my house has perhaps tripled. So I sell the home I purchased 30 years earlier at $250,000 for $750,000. Of this amount I pay a realtor (another middleman) 6% of the sale amount, plus my end of closing costs. Let's say this total comes to approximately $50,000. So I get a check for $700,000 and feel like I've made a killing. The truth is my house has actually cost me $20,000 in a down payment, $230,000 in principle loan amount, $525,000 in interest payments on the loan, $150,000 in repair, maintenance and home improvement costs, approximately $60,000 in real estate taxes and about $50,000 in closings costs and realtor fees bringing my total investment in my house to $1,035,000.

So when I compare what I have spent to what I make on the sale, I actually find that after 30 years of a lot of hard work I have lost about $335,000 on my house purchase. In short, I have spent 30 years working and for the most part working diligently for the money lenders and middlemen rather than for my own well-being.

Hell of system, isn't it? Throw in my car loan, my kid's college loan, the loan I have taken out for my business, a home improvement loan or two, maybe a periodic vacation loan, bank credit card interest payments, my retail store credit card interest payments, varying processing fees, late payment fees and more and I can accurately say that, like a mouse running on a wheel in a cage, I have spent the greater part of 30 or more years of my life exhausting my talent, my energies and my spiritual promise making those people who by talent, cunning, inheritance, criminal act, hard work, luck or some combination substantially wealthier than they were in the first place.

And if you still doubt the validity of my premise, here are a few other facts that may get your attention. Let's say you have a credit card on which you have a debt of $5000. And let's say your interest rate is 14%. If you pay only the minimum balance monthly it would take you around 25 years to pay off the full debt which, by that time, would be a total of around $12,500. And if, per chance, your credit score suffers a decrease during this period or you miss a payment even on an unrelated debt, your bank could increase your interest rate substantially and apply it retroactively. Nice business, right! Nice, ethical business!

I know this is a pretty cynical view of the way the money world works! But unfortunately, it is an accurate view. And yes, I also know that I too, by talent, cunning, inheritance, criminal act, hard work, luck or some combination of these factors can become one of those people who accumulate enough excess money to lend it to others at relatively high rates of return or I can invest my excess in the stocks of businesses that lend money or manipulate money to others and therefore I too can get rich. It's the beauty of our free enterprise system, isn't it, that anyone who wants to, within reason of course, can join the great usury and manipulation train?

Safeguarding These Few Precious Moments

Is there an alternative? Yes, I believe there are many, but the first and most important from my standpoint is that by significantly reducing the amount of usury a lender can charge and by altering the way we allow money markets (stock, currency, options, etc.) to manipulate its flow we can alter the very nature of how each of us currently spends what the poet Mary Oliver describes as these "few wild and precious moments we call our lives."

Does this mean stock exchanges, banks and lending institutions would no longer exist? No, it only means that they would be considered service organizations in the truest sense of the word. Their funds would enable businesses to come into being and individuals to acquire things that they truly need to live lives of greater effectiveness, but these lending institutions would not accumulate vast amounts of wealth in the process through excess interest charges nor would these interest charges dictate the way the rest of us as human beings have to live our lives.

Since we are on the subject of profit, I find no reason to stop just with the money lenders. We could also create a society in which the same thing would be true for all of us and for the companies we work for and the businesses we own. Just as we would limit usury, in this new America, we could also take a giant step forward by limiting greed as a primary motivation for doing whatever we do as individuals and as businesses. In short, we could prevent companies from entering or staying in the marketplace just to make a profit and in doing so, we would accomplish what for me are some remarkable and valuable results.

We would change and elevate the standards by which organizations evaluate their success. We would reduce the number of organizations that produce the same kind of products or that enter the market and produce inferior or shoddy products and deliver poor quality services just to make a buck. We would also, and here's the real kicker, allow most individuals to spend their lives pursuing very different goals than those that currently occupy them. People would, in fact, work to contribute to the betterment of life, but not live to work or be required to spend their lives working two or three jobs just to make ends meet and just to satisfy the profit motives of the money lenders, the money manipulators and the businesses that serve them. As a result the majority of us would only work as much as was necessary or as much as we choose and instead of being in servitude to usury we would have the opportunity to live, play, learn and explore other dimensions of human consciousness and existence instead of repeating the same old drama that has occupied man for so many centuries. We would, in fact, live in a world of genuine abundance rather than scarcity, a world in which we would have the opportunity to live more fully and work a lot less at least for other people's profit!

I know, of course, that the argument presented here is simplistic and leaves a number of primary dynamics within the free enterprise system unexplored, however, there is no doubt, at least in my mind and heart, that something is wrong with a system that places people in positions of economic servitude in order for them to gain access to the basic things they need – food, water, shelter, clothing and human interaction. There is something wrong with a system that arbitrarily allows some to continue accumulating much more than they require while the majority remain at or below substitute levels; that allows some to take personal possession of significant natural resources that are God given and not man made.

Chapter Fifteen
Providing Quality Healthcare

—〰—

"Nothing is politically right
which is morally wrong."

— Daniel O'Connell

It stuns me that a number of recent administrations feel entitled to continue strutting about on the world stage proclaiming us as the only remaining superpower and yet we rank 37th internationally in healthcare, 14th among the leading industrialized nations in education and 7th in the world in the longevity of our people. Imagine that, America the beautiful, America the powerful, America the technology giant, 37th in the world in providing quality healthcare to our people!

You know the story! At last count more than 50 million Americans are without healthcare. Count them! That's 50,000,000! That's one in four Americans! And this number does not include millions of seniors who are no longer employed, who fall under the barest minimum coverage provided by basic Medicare and Medicaid or who cannot afford either supplemental health coverage or RX prescription coverage. So in many ways this 50 million number is very low and misleading. Although I have not conducted my own study, when all is said and done I suggest there are at least 100 million Americans who are without adequate medical coverage and in this country that means there are 100 million citizens without adequate medical care.

And if any of the pompous voices in the White House or Congress object to this number and claim that Medicare and Medicaid are terrific programs, ask them when they last read a basic Medicare or Medicaid policy? Ask them if they have ever had to deal with the absurd layers of bureaucracy associated with either of these programs or if they would be willing to put the lives and well-being of their children, spouses and parents on the line under their provisions.

Slim to none, that's the most probable answer! The members of Congress, the Judiciary and the Executive Branch are covered under one of the most comprehensive healthcare plans in the world and you know what? It's paid for with our money! Yes, paid for with tax payers money and some of these tax payers include individuals in the 50 million category who do not have healthcare coverage themselves.

Facing Reality

So the question I have for you and for myself and especially for the folks in Washington is – How can we as Americans continue to live with the reality that so many of our fellow citizens are living each day at such risk? And please do not treat this as some kind of theoretical or hypothetical question. For just an instant, please close your eyes and put your-self in the place of one of these very real people who are in pain and cannot find relief; who suffer from chronic medical conditions and diseases and do not have the means of receiving effective diagnosis or treatment. Put yourself in their shoes and ask yourself what you would do if you had to make a choice between seeking medical help, paying for medication or eating. Or imagine yourself in the emergency room of your local hospital with your child or grandchild. Imagine waiting hours for someone to attend to their pain and then being told there is no room at the inn – not because the hospital can't treat this child, but because you don't have any or adequate medical insurance.

These are not theoretical instances! These are not hypothet-ical people! Instead these are very real people – your neigh-bors and fellow citizens – who face life and death choices like these every day.

From my perspective, it is not only unjust and incomprehen-sible, but insensitive and inhuman that we allow more than one quarter or more of our fellow citizens to live under such conditions and at such risk each day. Indeed, for a nation that prides itself on being so humane to people at risk in nat-ural catastrophes around the world, it is also hypocritical and unacceptable.

And this atrocity, this growing stain on the American soul, does not address other aspects of the healthcare coverage debacle that are negatively impacting our way of life and are quickly and surely leading us down a very serious and dan-gerous path toward becoming not just a second tier economic power, but perhaps just another footnote in history; another nation that lost sight of its purpose and vision and became another example of decline.

So what are these other aspects of our healthcare debacle I'm referring to? I am talking about all of the other hidden costs, the costs that few talk about when they address our healthcare system. One of these is the cost levied on the individual lives of many of our citizens who are forced to spend a very high percentage of their productive time earning enough money to pay for their medical insurance and most especially for all of the things that are not covered by their insurance.

I am also talking about the large number of our citizens who are forced to stay in dead end jobs for years with companies they don't respect or support simply to continue receiving healthcare coverage. Not only does this impact the passion and energy and value they express in their individual lives, it also detrimentally impacts productivity, performance and innovation and hence the quality of the goods and services we produce.

I am also talking about another serious condition that is the result of this healthcare debacle, the fact that more and more American companies, large and small, are finding it harder and harder to compete locally and internationally because the enormous cost of providing healthcare coverage to their workers is preventing them from being price competitive. I am talking about the fact that under our current system we, the consumers, in addition to paying ridiculously high costs for medical coverage, now have to pay higher costs for all of our goods and services as well.

Fixing What Is Broken

In short, I am talking about a healthcare system that is not just in need of a fix, but is broken; a healthcare system that is having a very detrimental impact on every aspect of our way of life! And yet every time there is an election, especially a presidential election, the candidates parade out the same old, limited, tired, partial and ineffective solutions. They bandy about terms like universal healthcare. They talk in emotional terms about all of the people who have fallen through the cracks and are not covered. Very high minded! Very inspiring and polite, but for the most part it is just talk and relatively bogus and ineffective talk at best!

This public debate about healthcare has been going on in this country since the late 1940's when England implemented a government sponsored healthcare system. When Canada, Sweden, and France implemented their own government sponsored plans, the conversation came up again and then again and again. In the late 1980's when Bill Clinton began making his early move toward the White House it came up again and then reached a relatively hot level of debate during the second year of his Presidency. But, of course, the concept of universal healthcare failed badly then – as it had at earlier times – and as a result it has been a political hot potato for the better part of 16 years.

Yes, whenever there is another presidential election it is again a hot topic, at least on the Democratic side of the debate. On the Republican side there is generally a deafening and frightening silence on this topic. No wonder polls show that most Republican candidates are not connecting with the public or that they are only connected to those members of the public who have coverage.

How did we create this healthcare debacle? And why in this so called proud land of ours, this land where individuals and local organizations and communities reach out to help one another in times of crisis, where we gather in church congregations to worship a compassionate God and donate our money, toys, food stuffs and more to the disadvantaged in other nations, where we go on elaborately planned missionary trips to other countries to build schools and establish medical clinics, why is this terrible and deplorable condition occurring here within our borders?

Adding Up the Real Cost of Greed

I have a one word answer to this question – greed! The medical insurance, medical services and pharmaceutical industries are held captive by a series of beliefs and practices that issue from fear and are based primarily on greed. They do not call it this, of course. In fact, many of the individuals who lead and work in insurance companies, hospitals and pharmaceutical companies do not consider what they are doing to be selfish or greedy at all. And many of them shouldn't. They are relatively decent people who are going about the process of leading their lives and earning their livings pursuing jobs and careers they believe are appropriate.

And, of course, their companies, associations and lobbying groups also vehemently deny this greed premise. They go on and on about all of the challenges associated with providing good coverage, of offering quality health services in hospitals, clinics and doctor's offices. They talk about how much of their profit is reinvested in the research and development of new drugs, new cures and the development of new equipment and services. But drugs, cures, equipment and services for what and for whom?

At other levels of these organizations, at the levels where policy is actually made, the arguments become more sophisticated, more aggressive and much more deceptive. This is the place where the free market economy and divine right of good and noble beings to accumulate enormous amounts of profit are defended with public relations campaigns about drug distribution programs in Africa or touring bus programs for a limited number of elders in the U.S. This is where lobbying efforts are initiated. This is the place where payoffs, political contributions, false and misleading advertising and massive public misinformation campaigns are authorized. This is the place where power is clung to with a tenacity that is truly amazing.

Among the messages that issue from these organizations, associations and lobbying groups are these – *"It's anti-American to have government healthcare and government sponsored insurance. Government sponsored healthcare will mean long lines and poor quality of service. Doctors will not want to be doctors. It would mean the end to innovation and the discovery of potential medicines and cures. It would put hospitals and doctors out of business."*

You know the stories. You've been listening to this verbal diarrhea for decades now. But as they say, *'if it walks like a duck and sounds like a duck, the probability is pretty high that it is a duck.'* And that is certainly true in this instance.

What is also true is that I do not have the time to fully explore the path we have taken to get here to this very troubling condition, nor do I have the time to recount all of the ways those who benefit most from the status quo keep us stuck in this awful place. I trust, however, that these few comments will add to the already overwhelming amount of evidence that is available on the failure of our healthcare and insurance systems in this country. I also trust that you already know that the rationales and arguments advanced by insurance companies, doctors, hospitals, medical equipment manufactures and pharmaceutical companies are, for the most part, simply not true.

We do not provide superior healthcare service in this country. We do a pretty good job of serving the needs of the upper middle class (shrinking dramatically in numbers daily) and the wealthiest, but we have a growing body of evidence to document the fact that more and more individuals of all economic classes do not receive adequate medical care. Studies also show that an increasing number of our citizens who enter our hospitals today run greater and greater risks of suffering some serious side effects, infection, misdiagnosis or death as a result of poorly trained doctors, overcrowded conditions, insufficient nursing personnel and shoddy services. And much of this is the direct result of decisions by companies who own hospitals to cut staff and services in order to generate higher profits.

It is also untrue that medical services provided in England, Sweden, Canada and France – to name just four of the 36 other nations that rank above us in providing healthcare – do not work very well. In fact, the vast majority of people in these and other countries report excellent medical services and also speak eloquently on the enormous relief they feel at not having to worry about how they are going to pay for their basic healthcare costs.

Looking At Some Alternatives

So what do we do about it? First and foremost, I think we should stop using tax funds to provide medical insurance coverage and medical care to our elected officials. Let's require them to go out into the same public marketplace that we do, shop around and find out for themselves what insurance companies offer and how they treat their average customers. We also have to stop sitting on the sidelines and leaving this debate to a relatively few political candidates who are promising us the world in order to get our votes and who, as soon as they are elected, go back to sleep on this issue. Instead we have to get involved and I mean now and in a big way. We have to stop allowing messages of fear about the risk of no coverage to motivate us to stay in jobs that do not serve us and in which we do not contribute in a meaningful way just to receive healthcare. We – those of us who are reasonably healthy and do not need immediate medical attention – need to raise a real stink with our insurance companies. Instead we need some kind of general strike or some collective movement to withhold our own insurance premiums for a while. Maybe we need to send our payments into a huge national escrow account with funds designated for eventual payment to our insurance company, but only after we have their attention. Yes, I know the thought of it scares you. *They will terminate my coverage and then where will I be!*

No they won't, not if we act in concert. They'll huff and puff, but the truth is they work for us and without our premium payments they would not exist even for a day. So maybe it's time we remind them in a language they understand very well that they are in business to serve us and they'd better start serving us or we will show them the door.

Getting Their Full Attention

Doctors? Hospitals? Medical equipment companies? Pharmaceutical companies? Same story! We need to get their attention right away and we can't do it individually. Only through a collective effort, only by mobilizing enough people and hitting them in their wallets can we wake them up. How do we do this? A good place to start is generating a lot of public noise. Let's start publicizing information about the profits these individuals and organizations make. Let's also do a much better job of showing our fellow citizens how the profit motive driving these individuals and organizations negatively impacts the range and quality of the services they provide. Let's disclose how much it costs – real and not inflated costs – to manufacture a specific drug or a piece of medical equipment or to deliver a specific medical service. Let's document the level of greed that is driving our healthcare and insurance systems and keeping these ineffective and failing systems in place. Let's look closely at the strategies pursued by companies that own hospitals and who cut staff and services to increase profits.

Let's also insist that our universities and schools institute new and more enlightened courses in medical ethics for doctors, nurses and other medical practitioners. Then let's require a body of experts, and not just from the medical establishment, to police the ethics and practices of all people who provide medical services. We also need to insist that our media present the real facts about the kind and quality of medical services that are available elsewhere in our own country as well as elsewhere in the world.

We need to eliminate or, at the very least, significantly reduce the amount of money people and organizations affiliated with the healthcare and insurance industries can contribute to political campaigns. We need to hold public hearings on the medical and insurance lobbying practices. We need to stop pharmaceutical companies from paying doctors to be their sales agents. We have to stop pharmaceuticals from paying for doctor and nurse continuing education programs. We have to flood the Medicare and Medicaid systems with complaints about doctor and drug costs. We have to find more attorneys who will file major class action suits against insurance and pharmaceutical companies. We must also take every and any opportunity possible to let elected officials and candidates know that we are tired of all of their procrastination, bullshit and lack of courage. We need to elect people who are willing to commit to finally getting the job done! And we need to challenge our doctors to rethink the reasons they entered their profession and to rediscover the enormous rewards above and beyond money that their skills hold.

Finally there is something each and every one of us can do each and every day. We can do all that we can to pay attention to what we eat, the amount of exercise and rest we get, and the amount of pollutants we remove from our home and work environments. We can also do all that we can to educate our children and those who do not realize that the best and ultimate antidote against these grievously ineffective, unfair and preposterously costly healthcare and insurance systems is good health. Yes, when we start spending as much time, effort, energy and money on preventative healthcare as we do on dealing with illness and disease once it occurs, we will be on the track to a more enlightened society.

Yes, in a new America, it is time to utilize our enormous talents, energies and resources to create a way in which every individual in this country and eventually around the world can lead healthy lives and get all of the medical support they require.

Chapter Sixteen
Honoring Our Elders

—ɯ—

"Life is too short to be small."

— Benjamin Desraeli

We are on the edge of one of the largest demographic shifts in the history of the world. By 2010 more than 50 percent of our population will be over 50 for the first time in recorded history. That means more than 140 million Americans – some 70+ million Boomers and almost 70 million seniors – will be firmly entrenched in the second half of life and dealing with all of its challenges, opportunities and implications. Combine this startling fact with several others – declining birth rates, increasing longevity rates, a shrinking tax base, startling technological and scientific advances, digital communications and more and the implications are astounding. They are astounding and also dangerous not just for the 140 million + people who are in or entering the second half of life at a rate of one every seven seconds, but for the millions of others here in this country and literally billions more around the world who will have to pay the price for the inattention and ignorance of our leaders in addressing the challenges this second half of crowd faces.

And make no mistake, this price will be heavy and it will impact every aspect of life. From healthcare and lifecare to design, construction, transportation, social services, support services, fitness, medicines, travel, apparel, technology, education. Yes, you name it and the consequences of this demographic revolution will be felt within this area.

Of particular consequences to those of us on both sides of the mid-life line here in the United States, our leadership – as it is and has been on so many other critical issues – is woefully inadequate and badly uninformed. In fact while the world is literally changing around us, our leaders have their heads down or buried somewhere else where the light of wisdom and vision does not shine. Instead they are focused on other things. What other things? You know – all of the habitual, short term, reactionary, aggressive, isolationist, power hungry, pork-barrel kinds of things.

As a result we are not at all prepared for this approaching demographic tsunami, and of even greater consequence we are, for the most part, not even aware it is coming.

Dealing with Our Fear of Aging

So what do we do about these challenges? First, we as individuals need to start dealing with our fear of aging and of death and turn toward the challenges and opportunities they represent rather than turning away from them. Next, through a literal avalanche of emails, letters and phone calls we need to insist that the President create a cabinet level post with extensive powers and a very large budget to assemble the best minds and hearts needed to fully understand the implications of this demographic shift and to articulate a range of possible solutions. And in case the President and Congress do not hear us, we need to turn off those faucets of campaign and political contributions and stop sending them our tax dollars until they do. As we all know, there is nothing like a rapid decline in available cash to get someone's attention.

Perhaps this new cabinet post should be named The Real Department of Homeland Security, for if we do not wake up to the reality of this brave new world that is coming, the external threats of terrorism will seem relatively miniscule by comparison.

What else can we do? Put a pin in the Myth of Youth by understanding, valuing and celebrating the characteristics and qualities associated with maturation and aging. We have, after all, seen the rather disastrous and insipid results that occur when we allow the inexperience of youth to have an unfettered rein in pop culture, rap music, science, technology, in government and especially in the media. While the enthusiasm, imagination and energy of youth may be laudable, there is also that other side in which their lack of experience and wisdom precludes them from modulating, discerning and refining options and possibilities. So we would be wise to again include the wisdom and experience of those of us who have been there and done that, those of us who are graying at the temples, may be sagging a little bit or a lot in some places and whose faces are lined and, God forbid, who even have age spots. We have to turn to the second half of life crowd and re-include our perspectives into the decision making mix. Yes, we also have to be willing to look life in the eye and to recognize that the movement into the later stages of life is as remarkable as the movement from birth and innocence into youth.

What else can we do? We have to begin expressing our outrage that we, one of the most powerful and economically
capable nations on Earth, allow our seniors to slowly
descend into lives of isolation and neglect. We have to start
being outraged over the fact that we allow our elders to end
their days in medical warehouses with insufficient and poorly trained staff rather than in remarkably inviting, engaging
and accommodating environments where they receive
excellent care. Yes, we have to finally admit that we are hiding them away instead of rewarding them at the end of their
long service with quality lifecare and alternative ways of
living. We are allowing them to fade away rather than taking advantage of their wisdom and applying it to the betterment of all.

Creating New Strategies and Forming New Alliances

Like some of the other wounds we discussed earlier, this
lack of attention to our elders will soon come back to haunt
us – especially those of us who are rapidly approaching
eldership ourselves. And if you are not yet in this second
half of life crowd, please do not underestimate the impact
this criminal negligence will have on those like you who
come after us, on those like you who will be required to pay
the enormous cost of supporting the health and lifecare
needs of more than half the population.

What else can we do?   We must attend to the implications
of this demographic shift at the regional, state and local levels as well. We must exercise our influence on our
Governors, State Legislatures, Mayors and City Councils, as
well as our leaders on the Federal level. We need to wake

them up about the impact the coming demographic tsunami will have on the economy of their governments. We need them to put cabinet level departments in place, forge bi-partisan alliances, and develop strategic relationships between government, non-profit organizations and businesses of all sizes in the private sector to address the challenges and develop effective alternate scenarios for the future. And just in case they choose not to listen, we need to stop paying their retirement plans and healthcare policies with our tax dollars.

We also need to prompt much greater awareness within our companies where workforce development issues and the long term impact of science and technology advances are causing very significant problems. With more than 25,000 people retiring every day in this country alone and with the push toward early retirement and buy out programs that represent the corporate response to the rising medical costs, organizations are losing significant amounts of their intellectual capital and placing additional and in some cases impossible performance issues on the remaining workforce. No wonder we are experiencing this mediocrity in products and this decline in innovation and services. How can we demonstrate excellence and regain our competitive footing on the world stage when we are understaffed, overworked and lacking the wisdom and experience older workers bring to the table?

We need to open a dialogue on aging and the implications of this demographic shift in our churches, schools, and local community organizations. We need to be better informed about the role each of these institutions and organizations can and will be required to play in the future. We also need to encourage the leadership of these organizations to develop their own alternate scenarios that speak to the effective use of their resources as the composition and size of congregations and memberships decline and the needs of these constituencies change.

We have to find a way to create a new, national training program for healthcare workers and service providers. We are already badly understaffed in both categories and the implications of this are truly frightening. Without qualified caregivers, the medical warehouse model will significantly worsen and the lives of our elders will become truly intolerable.

To this end, I think it would be prudent and effective to stop participating and fueling the ugly and acrimonious public debate on immigration that has been raging in this country of late and instead begin to consider the ways we can design new and more enlightened immigration policies with those countries in the world where the nuclear family is still in tack and the concept of nurturing has not yet been lost to the gods of commerce and progress. Perhaps we can establish immigration quotas and categories that will help us augment our needs for health and lifecare workers. Perhaps we need only wake up to the possibilities and we can solve one of the biggest challenges we now face.

Is there more we can and should be doing? As is the case with each of the challenges we have discussed in previous chapters, the real fix begins with each of us as individuals. We truly have to stop denying and start coming to terms with death and dying. We have to stop giving in to the inclination to hide from these realities in senseless forms of entertainment and obsessive forms of activity. Indeed, we cannot shop, eat, recreate, sex, surf the internet, play golf or work our way out of the undeniable and inevitable fact that we all will die.

Indeed, the only sensible and intelligent thing any and all of us can do is to come to terms with our own mortality, learn as much as we can about our choices and options, put our affairs in order, squeeze more of the juice from our past, transfer our knowledge and the fruits of our experience to others, and celebrate the life we have lived to date and most especially the life we have remaining.

We also need to be willing to learn from other cultures, religions and philosophies that do a much more conscious job of integrating death into life. And finally, we would be wise to take the advice of Carlos Castaneda, the writer of the Don Juan series, who tells us to *"Always keep death close at hand."* For if we befriend death; if we consult death, we have a much greater probability of leading more meaningful, heartfelt and purposeful lives.

Chapter Seventeen
Serving Our Young

—⁓—

"The surest way to corrupt a young man
is to teach him to esteem more highly
those who think alike
than those who think differently."

— Friedrich Nietzsche

If we are ever to claim the legacy of our founders and fulfill
the promise of democracy we must finally begin to truly
serve our young, not as I said in the prologue, by pacifying
them with trivial pursuits, poisoning them with junk food or
inducting them into forms of mental slavery to inconsequential forms of entertainment, addictive video games that promote death and destruction and the emulation of celebrities
and athletes who waste their precious gifts and degrade our
primary values. No we must educate, inspire, challenge and
motivate our children. We must encourage them to explore
their unique gifts and the distinct and individual contributions they have to make. We must encourage them to be

curious about life, both the external and internal dimensions of it. We must invite them to explore the unknown, the unique and the different. We must introduce them to art, literature, music and culture, not as occasional or optional topics, but as essential parts of their learning curriculum. We must teach them to journey into themselves, to know the landscape of their psyches and their emotions, their dreams and passions and their purpose. We must allow them to demonstrate their competence, to develop new skills and capacities and to push the boundaries of knowledge forward not only in what we consider practical areas, but in those areas that encourage the use of imagination, insight, intuition and creative expression.

Our children, you see, are much more than fodder for the great economic machine. They are much more than undisciplined energies that need to be pacified and controlled by encouraging their deeper emersion in foolish pursuits and gluttonous consumption. Our children are our hope for a future more remarkable and wonderful than our present and so we must provide them with quality education in content, values, the arts and especially in process over task. Who cares whether they get the right answers all of the time? Instead we must encourage them to experiment. We must invite them to explore, expand and experience. In short, as the old cliché goes, we must teach them how to fish rather than give them fish for in this way will be giving them the gift of self-sufficiency.

We must also offer them inspiring role models from whom they can learn to master the art of living sane and sustainable lives. And this education I am referring to is not the contemporary model that mistakenly substitutes the digesting of facts and information and their regurgitation for the real thing. No the education I am speaking about takes its meaning from the original Latin word – 'educare' – which means 'to call forth from within.'

Empowering Our Children

We need to teach our children how to be self-sufficient; how to call upon their own resources of body, mind and spirit; how to be curious, and how to access and rely on their own inner wisdom. We must teach our children how to access and celebrate their creative spontaneity. We need to teach our children to be unique not similar, to stand out as much as to fit in, to pay as much if not more attention to the promptings of their hearts as they do to the thoughts that we have tried to put into their heads. We need to encourage them to think for themselves, to understand the difference between believing and knowing, to be discerning and objective, to celebrate and thrive in the arts as well as in commerce, and above all, to celebrate the extraordinary energy that comes from living authentic lives that are aligned with their values and that call them forward toward higher degree of consciousness.

And this is just the beginning of what we need to do to serve our children. We need to create a new America in which when we proclaim 'no child left behind' we are doing much more than coining a politically convenient catch phrase or setting minimal targets to improve reading or math skills. In the new America we need to actually commit ourselves to invest the time, energy and resources needed in these young hearts and minds who are our best and only hope for advancing the highest goals for the future.

We, as adults, as parents, teachers, coaches, members of the clergy, public servants, corporate executives, celebrities, athletes, professional service providers, healers, artists and elected officials also have to stop modeling schizophrenic behaviors that have us practice one set of values and behaviors in the outside world and another set at home. Instead we must be willing to model an end goal for them that is balanced and whole. And if we are not yet able to do so in all ways and on all occasions, we should at the very least have the decency to encourage them to strive for the heights that we have not or cannot achieve. We also need to do our best to demonstrate honesty, integrity, mutual respect, collaboration and cooperation, and transparency. Yes, transparency. We must be open and honest with them about our failures as well as our successes. We must let them witness our process so that they can learn from the choices we make, the values we practice and the ways in which we employ whatever skills and abilities we possess.

Creating Radical Change

Yes, this business of serving our young is a big job. Too big, you say! Well, I say it is the best and most noble job any of us could ever do, a far larger and nobler job than most of the jobs that currently occupy us. But let us not make the mistake of thinking that our objective is to turn our children into our clones. Our objective cannot be to populate the world with more human beings like us. Surely enough of us have had more than enough of the kind of results we have visited upon the world. No, our job, as John Bennett, educator and musician, has suggested is to assist our children to *"be free from the past"* so that they can truly invent a new future.

And, as he pointed out, *"We can be free from the past only when we have so changed ourselves as to no longer be the same person who performed the original actions."*

So how do we change ourselves this radically? We must journey deeply into our own hearts. We must do the hard and sometimes painful work of acknowledging who we are, what we are currently doing and have done and the impact this doing has had on the people and world around us. In short, we must learn how to make peace with our past so that we can be free and able to live in the present and plan for a new future, one in which we are no longer the prisoners of unconscious, habituated behaviors and the unexamined beliefs we have inherited from previous generations. Our work is to lead our children, if not into a future that is new and fresh and full of unexplored opportunities and promise, then at the very least to the border of this new dimension.

How else can we change ourselves so radically that it makes it, as John Bennett has said, *"Impossible for us to act dishonestly."* We must have the courage to be open, to be vulnerable, to let go of what we already know so that we can become what we always dreamed we could be. If we work toward this end, even if we do not fully arrive at our destination, we will at least point the way for those who follow us.

Is there a better choice? I don't believe so. To continue to propagate our limitations in our children is unconscionable. Only by setting our children free from the shackles of ignorance, hatred, bigotry, selfishness, fear, distrust, violence and war can we hope to serve them. Only by allowing them to experience the truth of St. Theresa of Avila's words can we contribute to setting them free:

"Light in the soul

Beauty in the person

Beauty in the person

Harmony in the home

Harmony in the home

Honor in the nation

Honor in the nation

Peace in the world."

Chapter Eighteen
Becoming Responsible Stewards

—ιπι—

"Nature uses as little as
possible of anything."

— Johannes Kepler

Whether out of ignorance or intentional culpability, we have for the most part done a terrible job of fulfilling our role as responsible stewards of our habitat and the many species that reside here. Instead through our unconscious devotion to progress at any cost, through our arrogance, our ignorance and the mistaken belief that we are the owners and not the stewards of the Earth and its natural resources, through our naiveté that what we manifest is good as long as it is economically justified, we have brought our species and our planet to the edge of chaos and destruction.

Now, of course, we begin to sing the song of environmentalism and sustainability. Now suddenly everyone is talking about green products and green practices. But is this just 'Green Washing' and another public relations opportunity for politicians? Is it an inconvenient truth that interferes with business as usual, or is it really the beginning of our demonstration of our sacred responsibility and trust even if it means sacrificing levels of comfort, profit or habitual practices to protect, nurture and defend Mother Earth?

Is the green movement about a new America in which the incontrovertible interconnectedness between all members of humanity and with all other species on this planet is the basis against which the effectiveness of each and every policy, product, and practice is measured?

I believe it is too early to say, but fortunately there are signs of hope. There are signs that the average American is actually beginning to grasp – at least at a superficial level – the fact that what each of us does each day either wastes or preserves the dwindling supply of natural resources that are still available for us. We are waking up to the reality that what we do each day either pollutes our air, water and soil or contributes to their clean up.

This is not, as some of the more close-minded reactionary beings in our Government and sciences have suggested, some kind of misguided, romantic tree-hugger stance. No, this is a common sense stance. We either get this or it gets us! It's as simple as that! Indeed, the facts are now indisputable. Among them is the reality that we – humanity as a whole – dump over 70 million tons of global warming pollutants into the air each day. That's over 25 billion tons of pollutants annually. The facts are that people in the United States (approximately 300 million out of a world population of over 6.5 billion) utilize more than 25% of the world's total energy and contribute the same or a greater percentage of pollution.

The facts are that we are experiencing an unprecedented melting of the North Pole icecap and the shrinking of glaciers in Iceland, Alaska and in Antarctica. The facts are that some studies predict the complete disappearance of these icecaps in 25 years and others, including a recent U.S. Navy Study conclude that it could occur in as little as seven years.

Dealing with Frightening Implications

Staggering, don't you think? Dramatic and dangerous climate changes. Significant changes in the level of our oceans. Each bringing truly traumatic conditions. Indeed, we only need to consider the fact that more than half of the world's population lives within one mile of the coastline on every major landmass on the planet to get a glimmer of the impact on humanity that a 5 to 10 foot rise in sea level will have. The implications are frightening!

What is also of critical importance and frightening to understand is that much of this horrendous destruction has not been intentional. In short I do not believe there has been a conspiracy on the global level to willingly destroy our habitat. Instead, until recently, those who have contributed most to these deplorable conditions have done so mostly out of ignorance, indifference and self-focus.

Not any longer though! One would have to be living in Sleepy Hollow to avoid taking immediate responsibility for any and every act that further endangers life on this planet. So wherever we find a specific industry group – energy, automotive, pharmaceutical, etc. still clinging tenaciously to their old beliefs, to pushing products and services they know are harmful, and to intentionally attempting to cover their damage to the environment with clever public relations programs and sexy advertising messages (like clean coal), we should literally run their leadership and boards of directors out of town and replace them with people who are genuinely awake and committed to our well being. If we can't find such people, we should either nationalize the company or industry or we should shut it down.

And once again, if we find ourselves, as we so often do, with a President and Congress who are complicit in allowing the mistreatment of the Earth and the species who reside here, we must take immediate steps to impeach them. If the destruction of our habitat is not sufficient grounds for this then I do not know what is!

This is not some wild and crazy scheme. It is our responsibility as stewards of this Earth to stop the abuse and pillage of its resources. This is no longer something we can think and talk about. It is something we must do and do now! And if we fail to act in immediate and constructive ways then we will be complicit in this most criminal and fatal destruction of our habitat. Indeed, if we fail to do all that is necessary to protect our habitat, then the planet we loose will be our own!

There is another thing we must do. We must stop this insane and destructive use of fossil fuels. Not only does it pollute our habitat, it also leads to war and aggression, increases our trade deficit, undercuts our economy and underwrites the prosperity of countries who seek to destroy us.

As if this were not already enough justification to prompt us to become energy self-sufficient and to invent sources of clean energy, the money we spend in other countries is being used to purchase many of our key companies. Astounding, isn't it? We sit around on our spreading rear ends on our overly stuffed couches watching commercials that promote products and services that continue our addiction and dependency on fossil fuels while America is being sold. In 2000 alone, for example, over $400 billion worth of direct foreign investment was made in U.S. companies and that includes critical banking, telecommunications, chemical, high tech and energy companies. But who's counting!

Chapter Nineteen
Using Science & Technology Responsibly

—⁂—

"Knowledge without sense is double folly."

— Gracian

There is little doubt that America considers itself to be one of the world's leaders in science and technology. The fact that this is no longer true does not, of course, get much play in our media or in the minds of our leadership in Washington. Instead both groups live in the past and recount stories of days of old. They point to our land of abundance, they parade out our tired space shuttle exploits and wax poetic on our superiority in weapons production. They point to the obvious fact that we have been, until China emerged as the economic juggernaut, the largest consumer of every conceivable gadget, widget and product that emerges as the byproduct of science and technology. And in fact, one need only look at the plethora of ads in local media to verify the unprecedented availability of these downstream products and services in every corner store in America. Unfortunately consumption and creation are two different things; a fact that we and our leaders must eventually deal with.

But I want to call your attention to another and perhaps less obvious aspect of this science and technology topic, the topic of how little care and effort we expend in evaluating the long term impact of the off-shoots of science and technology on our health and well-being and on our environment.

In starting down this path I do not, however, want you to think that I am suggesting that in the new America I speak about I am opposed to our taking advantage of the products and services that result from our advances in science and technology. Instead, what I want us to do is to avoid becoming blind slaves to them.

To do this, I believe we need to become much more conscious of the long term impact these products have on our health and our environment and to avoid our inclination to act like children who have discovered a new toy. Instead we must learn to take a much more mature position and to do all that we can to identify and create a new public dialogue on some of the implications and impact the widgets, gadgets and advances that science and technology bring to us.

Indeed, unless we bring this kind of mature awareness into the game, we will find that our unfettered devotion to the byproducts of science and technology will continue to have enormous and dangerous consequence.

Ask the People

I know, all this sounds alarmist at best especially in this land where consumerism has been elevated almost to an art form. I mean, why would anyone be opposed to advances in technology and science? I don't know, maybe we should ask parents around the world who are finding their children becoming addicted to internet and forms of video gaming that are filled with images of death and destruction.

Maybe we should listen closely to teenagers who kill people and report that they are surprised when the individuals they shoot do not jump back up or morph into new forms as they do in the video games they play. Perhaps we should ask the children who are spending enormous amounts of time – as much as 8 to 10 hours or more a day – in virtual space living virtual lives and denying their real ones. Maybe we should look at the fact that the reading capabilities of many of our young people have dropped significantly or that as a result of text messaging there has been a dramatic degradation in the ability of our children to use their own language.

Maybe we should ask the hundreds of thousands of people who have suffered unwanted and detrimental effects from drugs supposedly designed to provide relief from particular illnesses and diseases but which have a list of side effects longer and more serious than the symptoms the drugs are intended to treat.

Maybe we should ask those who lose loved ones under the hands of incompetent medical practitioners who try out so called advances in equipment and medicines that have not been effectively tested. Maybe we should ask those who suffer the serious erosion of their health due to foods the FDA passes on to the public without appropriate, long term testing.

Maybe we should ask individuals and organizations all across the country who find themselves dealing with the toxicity – some of it with lifecycles hundreds of years long – in their homes, their places of work and worship and in the natural environment around them; toxicity that issues as an unexpected byproduct of many products that were supposedly created to make our lives easier and more effective.

Unfortunately, few if any of these products were tested by their manufacturers or by our watchdog organizations for long term impact. Instead, in the rush to market, in the rush to make a profit, these long term considerations were either never considered or were by passed. The result, a toxic waste dump of an environment and our inability to trust the companies that make our products to function at a high enough level of ethical standards to protect us.

To be fair, much like the comment I made in the last chapter about responsible stewardship of our habitat, a lot of this toxicity arises accidentally and not maliciously. That is, up till now! But there is much too much information out there now on the detrimental impact common household products, building products, industrial cleaning products, energy products, medicines and healthcare products have on all of our lives for anyone to deny the need to implement a very different system for birthing and testing new products, new serves and new technologies going forward.

Creating New Measurements

We have to wake up! We have to create new and more independent and mature evaluations, new testing procedures, a
much richer public dialogue and a much more responsible
public information system about the products and services
our science and technology produce. We must also hold
companies that are engaged in scientific and technological
research to rigorous standards of truth in advertising.

We certainly need to institute a complete overhaul of the
FDA and all other regulatory agencies. In fact, from my perspective and especially after the disastrous record of recent
administrations in contributing to the destruction of our
environment, the job of nominating people to run these
agencies, indeed, the actual job of running these agencies
should be taken out of the administration's hands and
returned to the public sector. By this I do not mean to imply
that the companies who do business in specific sectors
should take part in this process, for that clearly is what happened under the George W. Bush administration where the
very businesses that required regulation and oversight
became the source for personnel and policies for these oversight organizations. Staggering isn't it that our government
should be not only unethical, but unconscionable?
Staggering, isn't it that we should stand so silently by and
allow it to happen?

How should the leaders and members of these organizations
be selected? Perhaps we should select them through some
kind of electoral process in which they would have to
declare their beliefs and prove their competencies. Perhaps

the business of regulation should fall to the faculties of our leading universities who would nominate leading scholars and scientists to participate on these councils on a rotating basis. Perhaps there is another way, but one thing is abundantly and undeniably clear, we can no longer allow the organizations and agencies that protect the public good to remain under the influence and authority of any one political party or interest group.

Finally, of course, there is the question of our individual responsibility in regard to science and technology. This, after all, is where the rubber meets the road. If we wake up to the dangers as well as the advantages of our science and technology; if each of us commits to staying better informed and more involved in what products and services we allow into our lives and into our homes; if we demand higher standards from the companies we work for and the companies whose products and services we use; then and only then will any of the other changes we have discussed in this chapter have real impact.

In short, in the new America we must be awake, aware and conscious of what we do everyday in our lives. We must ask ourselves what our priorities are and discover if we are more interested in profit and so called progress at any price or if we are more concerned about the well being of our children and our environment, about the quality of our lives and the state of our health. We must ask ourselves if we are interested in continuing to be victimized by the viruses of fear, distrust and scarcity or are more interested in the power of truth and abundance. We must decide whether convenience is really so important that we will pay any price for it, including the destruction of our planet.

Yes, we have to wake up if we are ever to live lives in which we can contribute our talent and labor as responsible members of this society for the betterment of our families and the advancement of our individual lives and not in blind servitude to some false gods of science and technology.

Chapter Twenty
Living Our Values

—ⵡ—

"He who created us without our help
will not save us without our consent."

— Saint Augustine

When I was a boy of fourteen I was graced to meet a truly gifted and enlightened history teacher whose name was Mr. Harry Walker. This man's passion and love of his subject were obvious in his every word and in the remarkably creative ways he found to present history to us. No boring recitation of facts, dates, places and names. No, under his baton, history became a living, vital thing; a pulsing parade of humanity moving across the canvas of time. It became a multi-dimensional story of the extraordinary journey humanity has taken – even with all of its fabrications and distortions, its frailties and its follies. History became an organic record from which I began to learn of the astounding victories and accomplishments and the atrocious failures and wrong turns of my species.

As a result, here I am, these many years later in a state of amazement that we pay so little attention to this organic record and, instead, insist on repeating the same mistakes over and over again that have plagued and inhibited our progenitors.

Who can say why? Stubbornness! Stupidity! Arrogance! Resistance to change! The lies told by our progenitors about their exploits! These and other less than laudable traits and acts certainly contribute to our failure to learn the lessons history has to offer us.

But 'why' this happens does not, in the end, truly matter as much as 'how' we go about changing this denial of the wisdom gained by previous generations and how we go about reclaiming the genuine potential that this great nation has to offer its own citizens as well as our brothers and sisters who inhabit the rest of the world.

So as I said at the beginning of this book and in a number of places in the preceding chapters, I dream of a new America in which we celebrate integrity and champion each person's right to live a life of real meaning and purpose. For without this connection to true meaning and purpose we are like vehicles without fuel or our digital gadgets without batteries; not only are we prohibited from functioning, we are also just additional clutter on the landscape. And clearly there is enough clutter. Clearly we have more than enough people and stuff that does not work very well.

Reclaiming Our Pride Naturally

I also believe that the new America I dream of will be a land in which we reclaim our self-respect and pride as the natural byproduct, not of our military might or the purchase of loyalty with massive amounts of foreign aid or aggressive and bullying foreign policy, but as a byproduct of our everyday thoughts, words and deeds.

Yes, it will not be as a result of some major breakthrough, not through the efforts of some charismatic leader on a white horse, not through the identification of some silver bullet strategy that we will turn the ship of state away from the rocks and toward open water. Instead I believe it will be as a result of our willingness to align our thoughts, words and deeds with our best and highest values. In this way, and only in this way, will we ever rediscover the promise of this great nation!

So I dream of a new America in which all of our citizens understand the privilege and practice responsible participation in governance and who can be assured that it is their participation and not the decision of a politically appointed and philosophically biased court that will determine their future.

I dream of a new America, undivided, optimistic, imaginative, talented, compassionate, abundant, united, authentic, committed to genuine ethical leadership and to solving critical challenges and maximizing opportunities for all of the world's citizens; a new America that will fulfill the hope of our forefathers and, in close collaboration with people all across the planet, will finally turn this landscape of fear and distrust into a genuine Garden of Eden.

Will you dream with me? Will you remember that the future really does lie in our hands. Will you remember that we can, as Peter Drucker once said, invent it?

Chapter Twenty-One
An Open Letter to Political Candidates

—⁂—

"The administration of government
like guardianship
ought to be directed
to the good of those who confer
not of those who receive the trust."

— Cicero

Dear Political Candidate;

I believe Cicero was correct in his advice and that you and I and all Americans can learn a great deal from his council. I also believe, as I said at the beginning of this book, that the steps we take now and in the next period of our history could well be the most important and critical steps we have ever taken for they will determine if we continue this rapid and precipitous decline toward the end of a noble dream or regain our sanity and once again set this ship of state on a heading that will lead us toward a proud and positive future.

To that end, I believe that you, as a political candidate, play a critical role in this process and so I ask you to reflect carefully on some of the ideas presented in this book, in this open letter and, most especially, to pay attention to the messages that come from that quiet voice inside you that guides you to do the best and highest good.

In 1964 when Marshall McLuhan made his now famous assessment that 'the medium is the message' he was issuing a challenge to us to wake up and free ourselves from what he called 'the shackles of 19th Century perceptions and beliefs.' Unfortunately, it is clear that instead of waking us up to the dangers ahead, his comment seems to have become a self-fulfilling prophecy. Indeed, the 'media' of our time have not only become the message, but this message has, for all intent and purposes, succeeded in trivializing content, marginalizing meaning and anesthetizing most of the world's population.

Getting Lost in the Sound and the Fury

So I begin this letter to you who claim to want to serve the public good with the reminder that any attempt by you to speak into the noise of the current political debate on the contentious topics that seem to divide us will eventually doom itself. Indeed although there is a great deal of 'sound and fury' out there, you and I and an increasing number of other Americans know that this 'sound and fury' not only fails to advance the primary goal of uncovering and executing real solutions, it actually drives us away from the debate.

As a result, in the absence of real content and meaning, the only choice left to you, the candidate, is to continue to perform empty mimicry and to deliver poorly disguised platitudes and posturings; and the only choice left to us, the voter, is to either turn away from you and the entire melodrama (as so many of us have) or to evaluate you on inconsequential and subjective qualities – physical appearance, glibness, accent and mannerisms and the superficial answers you often deliver to what we all know are enormously complex challenges. Yes, with no other viable options available to us we, the people, like the bystanders along the parade route for the King Who Had No Clothes, turn a blind eye to the charade. How else could we possibly explain the fact that this or any other nation could elect so many mediocre and dramatically under-qualified individuals to public office?

Fortunately for us and for the particularly fragile balance of our world, however, even the heavily sedated eventually wake up and from my perspective, this waking up is happening for an increasing number of Americans. Yes we, the members of this Aspirin Culture, are showing signs of having had enough stumbling around numbly in the dark and although a clear strategy has yet to emerge by which we can find our way back into the bright light and sunshine of hope, there is a damn good chance we are moving in that direction.

Taking Advantage of A Rare Opportunity

As a result, I believe this waking up offers you a rare opportunity to participate in the creation of a new kind of political conversation in which you and all other candidates place a much greater focus on 'process' (how we can arrive at solutions) rather than on the solutions themselves. And I believe this shift in focus will gain you far more credibility as a candidate than your position on any single issues.

This focus on process will also point the way to the only sensible and successful means of actually uncovering the essential and effective solutions we require.

So my advice to you is to avoid repeating the same mistake that candidates and office holders have been making for so long – stop pretending you have 'the answers' to most of the major challenges we face. Instead start saying what everyone already knows – *These challenges are daunting and if we are ever to be successful in addressing them we have to find a new way of uncovering and implementing them.* (As the old saying goes – "If you always do what you have always done, you will always get what you have always gotten.") By this act alone you will both differentiate yourselves from the pack as well as serve the greater good.

Being Heard

As I said, I believe one of your primary challenges is to break through the information overload and to do so you must avoid being seduced into speaking into the current political conversation about surface (transient) issues and instead address the process itself. While this may seem impossible in the face of both the media's and the public's seemingly insatiable appetite for sound bites, each question asked about a surface issue becomes another opportunity for you to point out the superficiality of the current debate.

Example: "Good question and I think you will agree, a really complicated issue. While I have my own opinion on the subject and our team has done a terrific job of researching the topic, I think it would be irresponsible of me to give you one of those glib 15 second answers we've become accustomed to getting from our leaders. Instead, I think we should stop looking for band-aid solutions and accepting short term fixes and start bringing the best minds together from all sectors (and I mean the best minds in the world) to work on finding real and sustainable solutions to this and other problems. Don't you think it's about time we actually solve some of these things?"

Creating A Genuine Vision

I also believe you will contribute substantially to the creation of a higher level of political dialogue by crafting and articulating a much more comprehensive vision for America, one that identifies clear goals, articulates possible roles and responsibilities, sets realistic and measurable timelines and establishes clear metrics by which we can evaluate our progress. For example – rather than talking about education, healthcare, poverty, energy and the environment as individual priorities within the current paradigm of scarcity, divisiveness and limitation, I recommend you paint a new world view in which your objectives and values are of a different and higher order, your priorities more meaningful, and your ability to cooperate and collaborate identified as essential elements in making our daily lives more positive, meaningful, effective and satisfying.

Paint a vision of a future world with images, sounds and feelings that allow us to experience your vision; a vision that describes a world in which 'fighting terror, drugs and poverty' or struggling over the allocation of resources made scarce by artificial manipulations are neither the focus nor the obstacle to living lives in genuine peace and in a climate of abundance, prosperity, hope and enthusiasm.

Also articulate a vision that challenges us to rediscover our discipline and patience and to do the real work necessary to achieve this new state. Create for us a vision that is clear, understandable and resonates with our deepest and most sacred needs for happiness and well-being. Create a vision that give us hope and re-energizes us.

If you craft this vision artfully and deliver it solidly – especially in a book that you rather than a ghost writer write – your message will not be lost in the information overload or perceived as the ramblings of a Pollyanna, but instead will be heard as the message of a powerful, compassionate and capable leader who is committed to making a real difference at a critical time. One other thing I recommend, give your vision a compelling, captivating title and symbols that makes it easy to remember and serve as the metaphors for the process itself.

In framing this new political conversation I recommend you address bedrock beliefs (those stable, unchanging beliefs) the constituency identifies as malleable (have not yet made up their minds, but about which they have a strong desire to know more) rather than those transient surface issues so much of our media focuses upon and fixed beliefs (those on which they have intractable positions). Speaking to individuals about fixed beliefs only alienates them further. Also speak more about those beliefs that unite us rather than divide us.

I also recommend that you identify and only utilize 'intelligent' and 'viable' media such as public broadcast (radio and television), the internet and credible and viable journalistic sources that will allow you to conduct a genuine, in-depth conversation and give you the scope and opportunity to articulate it most fully. These kinds of quality media interactions offer you the only unique opportunities to amplify the reframing of the political conversation with any real dignity and depth.

I know this is not an easy task, however, if you articulate a compelling vision that explores a new and higher state of existence for America; a vision that identifies more viable roles for each and every American in fulfilling this country's destiny of bringing genuine democracy to the world, you will open the door to real, content-focused media.

Focusing On Process Rather Than Partial Solutions

As part of your focus on 'process' rather than giving glib answers and partially formed solutions, you can educate the public on the difference between discussion (from the Latin 'discutere') which means to shatter into pieces and dialogue (from the Greek 'dialogos') which means to arrive at truth through reason. I also suggest you model this difference whenever possible.

Example: "As most of you know, our normal form of public political debate doesn't work all that well. No wonder! It is based on what we call discussion. In discussion we take a topic, rip it into pieces, stir up a lot of emotions, go away unresolved and mad and generally stay that way – sometimes for a long time. I'm interested in finding a better, more intelligent way for people – even people who disagree – to be able to address the issues we face, identify our commonalities rather than focus on our differences, and use the resources that are available to us wisely and in concert so we can finally solve the problems we face."

Indeed, I strongly recommend you use every opportunity to stress the fact that the challenges we face are too complex for a small group of isolated and philosophically biased individuals from any one party or sector alone to solve. Point out that those who insist on band-aid, quick fix alternatives, who continue serving up simplistic solutions are apparently more interested in accumulating personal power and having their way than in finding real answers. Also point out that this inclination not only adds to our difficulties now, it also increases substantially the inevitable price future generations will all have to pay.

So whenever possible continue to stress 'process' over 'fix' by calling for the formation of special Brain Trusts, advisory boards and special study groups that bring our best and brightest from the public, private, corporate, research and academic sectors together (and don't limit the search to this country) to apply their talents, intelligence and resources to genuinely address our challenges. By this I do not mean the usual collection of tired old faces and equally tired minds who spend months haggling over the wording of so-called 'bi-partisan' reports that ultimately only put a vanilla face on a strictly partisan effort. I'm talking about a genuine collection of the best critical thinkers of our time, no matter where they come from or what political philosophy they represent. This will not only advance the 'process' proposition, it will also position you as an innovative, thought-leader and peer of the experts.

Issue Us A Challenge

I also strongly recommend that you use the complexity and immediacy of the many challenges we face, as a reason to issue a call to the rest of us. Challenge us to become participants and co-collaborators in making our world safe and sustainable. Remind us of Marshal McLuhan's quote about there being *'no passengers on Spaceship Earth, only crew members.'*

Also remind us of Emerson's sage advice, *"Talent for talent's sake is a bauble and show. Talent working with joy in the cause of universal truth lifts the possessor to a new power as a benefactor."*

Help us to remember all sorts of ways to get and stay involved from town hall meetings and innovative public opinion processes to participation in local community, church and educational organizations. Encourage us to redefine our responsibility as citizens. Describe for us the characteristics and qualities we and you need to develop and display in order to return trust and confidence to our political process.

Please also speak to one of the primary aspects this 'call' must contain – that we, as individuals, have to take primary responsibility for our lives and our nation back – back from the degrading values that erode our family structure and primary institutions, back from the arrogant and self-focused process we now call politics, back from the numbing sense of media addiction that overwhelms us and saps us of our energy, discipline and commitment.

Remind us that we have to do something about our addiction to noise and violence, to insipid forms of entertainment, to foods that kill us and fear based thinking that causes us to withdraw. Inspire us and tell us that we, like athletes, have to go into training in order to overcome the lethargy and indifference that has us in its grips. We have to get back in shape to get this country back on track so that it can fulfill the promise made in its founding documents to its people and to the world. I believe this is a call that will be incredibly well received.

And do not listen to the fears of the politically correct and the timid. Such calls to action do not turn us off, but instead thrill us and re-engage us in pursuits we know are higher and more worthy. In short, these calls re-ignite in us a sense of purpose and this purpose and commitment will serve this nation greatly.

Walk Your Talk

In addition, I believe the aligned demonstration and practice of a specific set of characteristics and qualities will greatly support you in your effort to reframe the political dialogue.

If you already possess and practice these qualities, then by all means continue to do so. If you find yourself lacking or deficient in some or all of them, then by all means use every means at your disposal to development and own them.

Authenticity

At all levels people are showing signs that they have had more than enough of those in the public eye who are out of touch with themselves, lack genuine conviction, and who therefore look to the shifting winds of public opinion as the primary source for their beliefs and strategies. My recommendation to you is to look instead for ways to stay in touch with your inner conviction and passion. This will, of course, become increasingly more challenging as the pace of the race and the demands for the articulation of positions pick up – an excellent reason for getting well grounded in this characteristic now. Authenticity (synonyms include: genuine, unique, sincere, original, bona fide) will also contribute more to your credibility and to the public's confidence in you in these troubled times.

While I believe strongly in coaching, I recommend that you avoid the kind of media coaching that places too much attention on body language, tonality and camera presence and not enough on genuine alignment, sincerity and content. It is the latter that will ultimately win the day. In short, I believe there is no substitute for originality and authenticity. And those who doubt it need only look to a number of individuals in our government today, both elected and appointed officials, to see how political campaigns devoid of genuine content and lacking in authenticity and originality result in the selection of individuals who lack both the skills and the character to lead us.

Honesty

In a climate such as ours in which distrust of public officials, corporate executives, the judiciary and the political process itself is at an all time high, directness and honestly will play like no other song. It will also bring a much needed breath of fresh air. To this end, I recommend you start early and remind the public often that we are all human, susceptible to error and that it is okay to not to know something. Indeed, remind us that it is actually a sign of courage, intelligence and a genuine commitment to get things right. (As Peter Drucker says, "There is a significant difference between doing things right and doing the right things.")

Also remind the public that 'no one can con an honest man' (i.e. as long as one is willing to admit what one does not know and has the perseverance to stay with it until things become clear, one cannot be taken advantage of). Unfortunately this did not apply to enough of the post 9/11 members of Congress. I believe this concept may, in fact, be one of the most important lessons any leader can remind us of at this time when our democracy is on the line.

Clarity & Common Sense

In line with honesty, keep things simple and communicate them in ways that resonate with common sense. It will prove an unbeatable combination – especially in this age of double-speak, spin and obfuscation. It will also be taken as a sign by the large number of citizens who have turned away from the political process that it is safe to come out and play again. Finally, it will remind us that even in this world of unprecedented scientific and technological advances and very complex issues, the greatest wisdom is and has always been spoken in plain language and through ideas and concepts that resonate naturally with our inner knowing.

Transparency

The first rule of both comedy and effective communication is – *Tell them what you are going to do. Do it. And then tell them what you have done.* Although this strategy has worked since the beginning of time, a lot of contemporary political candidates and office holders seem to believe that doing what they want to do, telling us something we might believe (for a while) and then denying what they have said and done when the pigeons come home to roost is a better formula. Clearly this kind of thinking is getting old. In this age of instant communication, emerging new constituencies, blogs, and a genuinely troubled populace, transparency will prove far more effective and attractive to the public.

Trust

We have already talked about the level of distrust, anger and cynicism present in our world today. Demonstrating the characteristics identified in this section will cultivate a new level of trust for you and contribute to re-establishing a strong relationship between you and the constituency you seek to serve. And trust in leadership will certainly be required if we are to successfully make the tough decisions, sacrifices and ultimately, the changes that are needed. (For more information on this it might be helpful to review John von Neumann's work on Game Theory – specifically the 'w' factor.)

Caring and Compassion

An old cliché tells us, 'no one cares how much we know until they know we how much care.' It is easy to trivialize this message and to suggest that it is something for the naïve and inexperienced to hold onto – which is precisely what many who make their way to power have done for so long. Reverse this trend and demonstrate genuine caring, empathy and concern for the people (as peers) and I believe the results, especially in this age of distrust and cynicism will astound.

To accomplish this, of course, requires the modeling of the characteristics/qualities discussed in this section, and two more: humility and the willingness to share one's vulnerability. The inability to demonstrate these two characteristics was, in my opinion, (voting improprieties aside) the factor that actually led to the defeat of both Al Gore and John Kerry. Had either been able to connect on a deeper and more caring level with the electorate and to demonstrate genuine empathy for the human condition, not from above the fray, but as people who were right in the thick of it with us, both elections would not have been close enough to have prevented manipulated courts and fraudulent polling place results to even matter.

Flexibility

At no time in history has this quality been more absent or more needed than it is today. Rigid, inflexible thinking, stubbornness and the unwillingness to reverse position or let go of previously held limited beliefs account for most of the world's primary problems. We see this in the halls of government, in boardrooms, church rooms, classrooms and living rooms and in our own bathroom mirrors. To model flexibility, to admit fallibility and to proclaim that revising one's position based on new findings and better insights is not only natural, but a sign of maturity and intelligence will pay enormous dividends for you as a candidate. Modeling this characteristic/quality will also greatly assist you to advance the state of the state at all levels of our society.

Humanity

Closely allied with caring is the need to demonstrate a genuine sense of humanity. And by this I do not mean the overly sentimentalized, manipulated forms of melodrama that have been badly abused by recent administrations. Instead I mean a deeply felt and emotionally communicated sense that we are not only in this together, but that whatever happens to the least of us happens to all of us. A genuine sense of humanity, of course, requires leaders to check their egos and any inflated sense of special entitlement and importance at the door. (See Robert Fuller on Rankism.)

It also requires that we finally do what McLuhan advised us – *give up our attachment to 19th Century perceptions and beliefs* – especially those that espouse the idea of 'the white man's burden' or the 'divine right of kings' (presidents, corporate leaders, theologians, etc.)

Celebration and Humor

No two characteristics are more absent in contemporary public life than celebration and humor. Indeed, it appears that most politicians believe that 'seriousness is next to Godliness and there ain't nothing next to that!' This does not imply that I think we should make light of the serious challenges we face, or that we should, as George W. Bush did, run up the flag arbitrarily and call the game victorious long before it is over. What I do believe, however, is that we need to stop trying to make ourselves important by being somber and stop believing that we somehow will drain our resolve by stopping along the way to laugh at our foibles and celebrate our courage, our willingness, our compassion and our incremental achievements.

Instead a strong sense of humanity allows us to admit our frailties while also acknowledging our remarkable and indomitable spirit. In this election, I believe humor and celebration will prove to be incredible allies to the candidate who uses them.

Reach Out to New Constituencies

I also believe that one of the most important things you or any candidate can do is to build rapport with the new constituencies which are for the most part ignored or underestimated by politicians.

What defines the largest of these constituencies? Oddly enough, the one obvious thing most political strategists constantly overlook – people! I know, it sounds ridiculous, but it is true. People and not beliefs are the genuine foundation for the truest constituency. And although people may be divided over surface issues, they are actually far more united on the things that really matter – bedrock issues and fundamental values.

After more centuries of divisiveness, domination, rape, pillage, planetary abuse and both political and religious warfare than any of us care to relive or remember, people are finally being forced by climate change, unprecedented environmental threats, the squandering of natural resources, a dramatically aging world population, the decline in birth rates in most industrialized countries and the new forms of terrorism that make the defense of national boundaries almost impossible, to admit that we are all members of the same species occupying the same habitat, and challenged by the same dangers. Indeed a growing number of us are finally admitting that we are not only interdependent, but inextricably interconnected when it comes to both our well-being and our survival.

This coalescing of smaller constituencies into a much larger, common constituency, although reasonably new, will soon force us to move outside the arbitrary boundaries of current labels – liberals and conservatives, blacks and whites, majorities and minorities, Christians, Jews, Buddhists and Muslims. Indeed, although the climate of fear and manipulation used by recent administrations may be rivaled by only a few other governments in history, the insufficiency of these labels to define and contain today's true constituency is becoming clearer.

Unfortunately, the major political parties and most political candidates do not seem to be benefiting from this knowledge. Instead they continue to attempt to shape their message to woo constituencies they believe have actual and unbridgeable differences. Even though the difference between the number of Democrats and Republicans who voted in recent elections was relatively slight, this fact has not served the parties sufficient notice or, if it has, this information has not prompted them to dramatically realign their strategies.

Instead they continue to scramble to grab just enough of their opponent's share of the pie to allow them to squeak by. Talk about lack of vision and a poverty consciousness!

So I recommend you become a lot more expansive and adventurous in your reach and recognize that the whole pie is available to whoever creates a new political conversation, especially a conversation that finally and adequately addresses bedrock issues and seeks to unify rather than divide.

A case in point! Numerous academic and think-tank studies over several decades have attempted to identify factors that prompt one to lean toward becoming a liberal or a conservative. Depending on the bias of the researchers, of course, the findings are generally advanced in terms that cause one side or the other to take offense. For example, some studies suggest that liberals are more flexible and conservatives more rigid. Others posture that liberals are only interested in social justice and fairness, while conservatives steer by a much stronger moral compass and in the process uphold the stability of traditions, the sacredness of life and, of course, the legacy of the republic.

What continues to astound me is that it seems so difficult for many candidates and office holders to articulate a political agenda that speaks as equally to those who believe in social justice and fairness and as it does to those who adhere to what they perceive as a stronger moral code and greater support for the sacredness of life. Are we not talking about human beings here – about the one and only true constituency? And are we not capable of taking Einstein's sage advice to "seek solutions to the problems we have created at a higher altitude than the one on which we created the problems" – a higher level on which our commonalities are much more natural and easy to find than our differences?

So my recommendation here is that in framing a new political conversation, avoid staying within the boundaries and divisions by which current constituencies are defined. Point out the detrimental impact fear-based thinking contributes. Instead go to a higher moral or ethical level and from there articulate an agenda that reframes our national priorities, redefines our goals and speaks directly to the heart of the human constituency, a heart that is bigger than the labels and longs to be reunited.

In doing this, the scope, common sense, naturalness and intelligence of a new vision will expose the positions and beliefs others are putting forward for what they are – misguided, misdirected and pale by comparison.

In my opinion, here are a few examples of new and unclaimed constituencies:

Boomers/Seniors

Today between 120 and 140 million Americans are either in or rapidly approaching the second half of life. That includes between 50 and 70 million baby boomers and over 70 million seniors who make up this highly influential and affluent segment of the population. In fact, by the year 2010 more than 50% of our population will be over 50 for the first time in history.

What makes this new constituency so influential? They have average incomes ranging from $75,000 to $250,000 + per year. Baby boomers alone earn more than $2 trillion annually. Together these two groups control 80% of the nation's financial assets, spend $750 billion annually, have 2.5 times the per capita discretionary spending power of younger households, spend $75 billion on healthcare insurance, $79 billion on new car purchases, 40% more than any other segment on travel and 74% more on vacations, purchase 35% of all new apparel, buy 41% of all personal care products, and spend $152 billion on healthcare.

So why is no one addressing the primary issues that impact this group today and will require their complete focus in the very near – healthcare, alternative community, ownership and lifestyle choices, legacy concerns, workforce productivity, the brain drain and hundreds of other issues that are melding this very powerful and influential segment of the population into a new constituency? Because our government and most of our institutions have had their heads down mucking around in old paradigm thinking, political posturing and wrong priorities for so long they haven't had the time to even name let alone begin to begin to address the legitimate concerns and needs of this group of approximately 140 million Americans.

And yet there is a population tsunami coming that will impact always every aspect of life from the way we design and deliver healthcare to the way we pay for it; from the kinds of products and services we make and deliver, to the way we design, fund and utilize public buildings and private residences. Yes, all this and more, and neither our current leadership nor any of the major candidates are talking directly about it.

Cultural Creatives

There is also a segment of the public defined by social researchers, Paul Ray and Sherry Anderson as 'The Cultural Creatives.' Estimates suggest this constituency is comprised of between 30 and 50 million Americans who share similar sets of values and needs. Themes like sustainability, environmental consciousness, carbon neutrality and many more resonate with this constituency because these topics represent bedrock issues for them. These topics, of course, are covered in a number of current political hot topics. What is not as apparent is that 'Cultural Creatives' seek for much greater meaning and purpose and define one of their long term objectives in terms of spiritual focus rather than materialism.

According to Ray and Anderson, this new constituency constitutes one of the fastest growing and most influential in the world. While there is overlap with the Boomers and other constituencies, learning more about the needs, desires and preferences of this group will prove to be particularly important in this election.

Transpartisan Movement

There is another emerging constituency – what today is being called the 'Transpartisan Movement.' Still small, of course, by comparison to the others and certainly marginalized by most party regulars, this emerging group, however, is I believe the harbinger of a shift in consciousness in the population at large that recognizes the need to find connections and bridges between seemingly boundaried constituencies rather than differences. From the signs present in the most recent election, candidates dismiss this growing constituency at their own peril.

Destiny Seekers

From the late 1960's through the early 1990's, there were a number of seminar companies in the U.S. who designed and created multiple day programs that assisted people to look at their lives, beliefs, and habitual practices.   Lifespring, est (now Landmark), Actualizations, Insight, The Summit and a host of others graduated millions of people.   Awareness, responsibility and contribution were some of the primary principles presented and encouraged in these programs, and in addition these organizations also managed to train some of the best and most dedicated volunteers in the country. To a large degree, the graduates of these programs constitute a small army of highly committed people who have not, to my knowledge, ever been adequately addressed or tapped by any one candidate. Familiarity with their language and metaphors and the primary values that move them can prove valuable. In addition, developing a focused effort to either enroll people from this constituency in the campaign or to discover who on the campaign staff may have access to one of more of the sub-groups within this 'transformational graduate community' could also be of significant value. A small army of highly trained volunteers is, as you know, not easy to come by. A number of these organizations, although less powerful than they were, are still operating.

It is my belief that all four of these constituencies will find natural affinity with the kind of 'Vision For America' discussed in this document.

In concluding, I can ask you once again to take the time to reflect on some of the ideas and recommendations presented here in these pages and above all, that you go into the quiet of your being and listen to the wisdom that awaits you there. I ask you to remember, as William Graham Sumner reminded us that, *"The real danger of democracy is that the classes which have power will assume all the rights and reject all of the duties – that is – they will use the political power to plunder others."*

The challenges we face demand a new and higher quality of leader. Are you prepared for these challenges? Are you one of the new leaders who can represent the well being of this nation going forward? Are you prepared to participate in the next American Revolution? Will you dream with us?

"Be the change you want to see in the world."
— *Gandhi*

The Declaration of Independence

The unanimous Declaration of the thirteen united States of America, When in the Course of human events, it becomes necessary for one people to dissolve the political bands which have connected them with another, and to assume among the powers of the earth, the separate and equal station to which the Laws of Nature and of Nature's God entitle them, a decent respect to the opinions of mankind requires that they should declare the causes which impel them to the separation.

We hold these truths to be self-evident, that all men are created equal, that they are endowed by their Creator with certain unalienable Rights, that among these are Life, Liberty and the pursuit of Happiness. – That to secure these rights, Governments are instituted among Men, deriving their just powers from the consent of the governed, – That whenever any Form of Government becomes destructive of these ends, it is the Right of the People to alter or to abolish it, and to institute new Government, laying its foundation on such principles and organizing its powers in such form, as to them shall seem most likely to effect their Safety and Happiness. Prudence, indeed, will dictate that Governments long established should not be changed for light and transient causes; and accordingly all experience hath shewn, that mankind are more disposed to suffer, while evils are sufferable, than to right themselves by abolishing the forms to which they are accustomed. But when a long train of abuses and usurpations, pursuing invariably the same Object evinces a design to reduce them under absolute Despotism, it is their right, it is their duty, to throw off such Government, and to provide new Guards for their future security. – Such has been the patient sufferance of these Colonies; and such is now the necessity which constrains them to alter their former Systems of Government. The history of the present King of Great Britain is a history of repeated injuries and usurpations, all having in direct object the establishment of an absolute Tyranny over these States. To prove this, let Facts be submitted to a candid world.

■ *He has refused his Assent to Laws, the most wholesome and necessary for the public good.*

■ *He has forbidden his Governors to pass Laws of immediate and pressing importance, unless suspended in their operation till his Assent should be obtained; and when so suspended, he has utterly neglected to attend to them.*

■ *He has refused to pass other Laws for the accommodation of large districts of people, unless those people would relinquish the right of Representation in the Legislature, a right inestimable to them and formidable to tyrants only.*

■ *He has called together legislative bodies at places unusual, uncomfortable, and distant from the depository of their public Records, for the sole purpose of fatiguing them into compliance with his measures.*

■ *He has dissolved Representative Houses repeatedly, for opposing with manly firmness his invasions on the rights of the people.*

■ He has refused for a long time, after such dissolutions, to cause others to be elected; whereby the Legislative powers, incapable of Annihilation, have returned to the People at large for their exercise; the State remaining in the mean time exposed to all the dangers of invasion from without, and convulsions within.

■ He has endeavored to prevent the population of these States; for that purpose obstructing the Laws for Naturalization of Foreigners; refusing to pass others to encourage their migrations hither, and raising the conditions of new Appropriations of Lands.

■ He has obstructed the Administration of Justice, by refusing his Assent to Laws for establishing Judiciary powers.

■ He has made Judges dependent on his Will alone, for the tenure of their offices, and the amount and payment of their salaries.

■ He has erected a multitude of New Offices, and sent hither swarms of Officers to harass our people, and eat out their substance.

■ He has kept among us, in times of peace, Standing Armies without the Consent of our legislatures.

■ He has affected to render the Military independent of and superior to the Civil power.

■ He has combined with others to subject us to a jurisdiction foreign to our constitution, and unacknowledged by our laws; giving his Assent to their Acts of pretended Legislation:

- For Quartering large bodies of armed troops among us:

- *For protecting them, by a mock Trial, from punishment for any Murders which they should commit on the Inhabitants of these States:*

- *For cutting off our Trade with all parts of the world:*

- *For imposing Taxes on us without our Consent:*

- *For depriving us in many cases, of the benefits of Trial by Jury:*

- *For transporting us beyond Seas to be tried for pretended offenses*

- *For abolishing the free System of English Laws in a neighboring Province, establishing therein an Arbitrary government, and enlarging its Boundaries so as to render it at once an example and fit instrument for introducing the same absolute rule into these Colonies:*

- *For taking away our Charters, abolishing our most valuable Laws, and altering fundamentally the Forms of our Governments:*

- *For suspending our own Legislatures, and declaring themselves invested with power to legislate for us in all cases whatsoever.*

■ *He has abdicated Government here, by declaring us out of his Protection and waging War against us.*

■ *He has plundered our seas, ravaged our Coasts, burnt our towns, and destroyed the lives of our people.*

■ *He is at this time transporting large Armies of foreign Mercenaries to complete the works of death, desolation and tyranny, already begun with circumstances of Cruelty*

& perfidy scarcely paralleled in the most barbarous ages, and totally unworthy the Head of a civilized nation.

- *He has constrained our fellow Citizens taken Captive on the high Seas to bear Arms against their Country, to become the executioners of their friends and Brethren, or to fall themselves by their Hands.*

- *He has excited domestic insurrections amongst us, and has endeavored to bring on the inhabitants of our frontiers, the merciless Indian Savages, whose known rule of warfare, is an undistinguished destruction of all ages, sexes and conditions.*

In every stage of these Oppressions We have Petitioned for Redress in the most humble terms: Our repeated Petitions have been answered only by repeated injury. A Prince whose character is thus marked by every act which may define a Tyrant, is unfit to be the ruler of a free people.

Nor have We been wanting in attentions to our British brethren. We have warned them from time to time of attempts by their legislature to extend an unwarrantable jurisdiction over us. We have reminded them of the circumstances of our emigration and settlement here. We have appealed to their native justice and magnanimity, and we have conjured them by the ties of our common kindred to disavow these usurpations, which, would inevitably interrupt our connections and correspondence. They too have been deaf to the voice of justice and of consanguinity. We must, therefore, acquiesce in the necessity, which denounces our Separation, and hold them, as we hold the rest of mankind, Enemies in War, in Peace Friends.

We, therefore, the Representatives of the united States of

America, in General Congress, Assembled, appealing to the Supreme Judge of the world for the rectitude of our intentions, do, in the Name, and by Authority of the good People of these Colonies, solemnly publish and declare, That these United Colonies are, and of Right ought to be Free and Independent States; that they are Absolved from all Allegiance to the British Crown, and that all political connection between them and the State of Great Britain, is and ought to be totally dissolved; and that as Free and Independent States, they have full Power to levy War, conclude Peace, contract Alliances, establish Commerce, and to do all other Acts and Things which Independent States may of right do. And for the support of this Declaration, with a firm reliance on the protection of divine Providence, we mutually pledge to each other our Lives, our Fortunes and our sacred Honor.

The Constitution of The United States

𝕸𝖊 𝖙𝖍𝖊 𝕻𝖊𝖔𝖕𝖑𝖊 of the United States, in Order to form a more perfect Union, establish Justice, insure domestic Tranquility, provide for the common defense, promote the general Welfare, and secure the Blessings of Liberty to ourselves and our Posterity, do ordain and establish this Constitution for the United States of America.

ARTICLE. I.

SECTION. 1.

All legislative Powers herein granted shall be vested in a Congress of the United States, which shall consist of a Senate and House of Representatives.

SECTION. 2.

The House of Representatives shall be composed of Members chosen every second Year by the People of the several States, and the Electors in each State shall have the Qualifications requisite for Electors of the most numerous Branch of the State Legislature.

No Person shall be a Representative who shall not have attained to the Age of twenty five Years, and been seven Years a Citizen of the United States, and who shall not, when elected, be an Inhabitant of that State in which he shall be chosen.

Representatives and direct Taxes shall be apportioned among the several States which may be included within this Union, according to their respective Numbers, which shall be determined by adding to the whole Number of free Persons, including those bound to Service for a Term of Years, and excluding Indians not taxed, three fifths of all other Persons. The actual Enumeration shall be made within three Years after the first Meeting of the Congress of the United States, and within every subsequent Term of ten Years, in such Manner as they shall by Law direct. The Number of Representatives shall not exceed one for every thirty Thousand, but each State shall have at Least one Representative; and until such enumeration shall be made, the State of New Hampshire shall be entitled to choose three, Massachusetts eight, Rhode-Island and Providence Plantations one, Connecticut five, New-York six, New Jersey four, Pennsylvania eight, Delaware one, Maryland six, Virginia ten, North Carolina five, South Carolina five, and Georgia three.

When vacancies happen in the Representation from any State, the Executive Authority thereof shall issue Writs of Election to fill such Vacancies.

The House of Representatives shall choose their Speaker and other Officers; and shall have the sole Power of Impeachment.

SECTION. 3.
The Senate of the United States shall be composed of two

Senators from each State, chosen by the Legislature thereof for six Years; and each Senator shall have one Vote.

Immediately after they shall be assembled in Consequence of the first Election, they shall be divided as equally as may be into three Classes. The Seats of the Senators of the first Class shall be vacated at the Expiration of the second Year, of the second Class at the Expiration of the fourth Year, and of the third Class at the Expiration of the sixth Year, so that one third may be chosen every second Year; and if Vacancies happen by Resignation, or otherwise, during the Recess of the Legislature of any State, the Executive thereof may make temporary Appointments until the next Meeting of the Legislature, which shall then fill such Vacancies.

No Person shall be a Senator who shall not have attained to the Age of thirty Years, and been nine Years a Citizen of the United States, and who shall not, when elected, be an Inhabitant of that State for which he shall be chosen.

The Vice President of the United States shall be President of the Senate, but shall have no Vote, unless they be equally divided.

The Senate shall choose their other Officers, and also a President pro tempore, in the Absence of the Vice President, or when he shall exercise the Office of President of the United States.

The Senate shall have the sole Power to try all Impeachments. When sitting for that Purpose, they shall be on Oath or Affirmation. When the President of the United

States is tried, the Chief Justice shall preside: And no Person shall be convicted without the Concurrence of two thirds of the Members present.

Judgment in Cases of Impeachment shall not extend further than to removal from Office, and disqualification to hold and enjoy any Office of honor, Trust or Profit under the United States: but the Party convicted shall nevertheless be liable and subject to Indictment, Trial, Judgment and Punishment, according to Law.

SECTION. 4.

The Times, Places and Manner of holding Elections for Senators and Representatives, shall be prescribed in each State by the Legislature thereof; but the Congress may at any time by Law make or alter such Regulations, except as to the Places of choosing Senators.

The Congress shall assemble at least once in every Year, and such Meeting shall be on the first Monday in December, unless they shall by Law appoint a different Day.

SECTION. 5.

Each House shall be the Judge of the Elections, Returns and Qualifications of its own Members, and a Majority of each shall constitute a Quorum to do Business; but a smaller Number may adjourn from day to day, and may be authorized to compel the Attendance of absent Members, in such Manner, and under such Penalties as each House may provide.

Each House may determine the Rules of its Proceedings, punish its Members for disorderly Behavior, and, with the Concurrence of two thirds, expel a Member.

Each House shall keep a Journal of its Proceedings, and from time to time publish the same, excepting such Parts as may in their Judgment require Secrecy; and the Yeas and Nays of the Members of either House on any question shall, at the Desire of one fifth of those Present, be entered on the Journal.

Neither House, during the Session of Congress, shall, without the Consent of the other, adjourn for more than three days, nor to any other Place than that in which the two Houses shall be sitting.

SECTION. 6.

The Senators and Representatives shall receive a Compensation for their Services, to be ascertained by Law, and paid out of the Treasury of the United States. They shall in all Cases, except Treason, Felony and Breach of the Peace, be privileged from Arrest during their Attendance at the Session of their respective Houses, and in going to and returning from the same; and for any Speech or Debate in either House, they shall not be questioned in any other Place.

No Senator or Representative shall, during the Time for which he was elected, be appointed to any civil Office under the Authority of the United States, which shall have been created, or the Emoluments whereof shall have been increased during such time; and no Person holding any Office under the United States, shall be a Member of either House during his Continuance in Office.

SECTION. 7.

All Bills for raising Revenue shall originate in the House of

Representatives; but the Senate may propose or concur with Amendments as on other Bills.

Every Bill which shall have passed the House of Representatives and the Senate, shall, before it become a Law, be presented to the President of the United States: If he approve he shall sign it, but if not he shall return it, with his Objections to that House in which it shall have originated, who shall enter the Objections at large on their Journal, and proceed to reconsider it. If after such Reconsideration two thirds of that House shall agree to pass the Bill, it shall be sent, together with the Objections, to the other House, by which it shall likewise be reconsidered, and if approved by two thirds of that House, it shall become a Law. But in all such Cases the Votes of both Houses shall be determined by yeas and Nays, and the Names of the Persons voting for and against the Bill shall be entered on the Journal of each House respectively. If any Bill shall not be returned by the President within ten Days (Sundays excepted) after it shall have been presented to him, the Same shall be a Law, in like Manner as if he had signed it, unless the Congress by their Adjournment prevent its Return, in which Case it shall not be a Law.

Every Order, Resolution, or Vote to which the Concurrence of the Senate and House of Representatives may be necessary (except on a question of Adjournment) shall be presented to the President of the United States; and before the Same shall take Effect, shall be approved by him, or being disapproved by him, shall be repassed by two thirds of the Senate and House of Representatives, according to the Rules and Limitations prescribed in the Case of a Bill.

SECTION. 8.

The Congress shall have Power To lay and collect Taxes, Duties, Imposts and Excises, to pay the Debts and provide for the common Defense and general Welfare of the United States; but all Duties, Imposts and Excises shall be uniform throughout the United States;

To borrow Money on the credit of the United States;

To regulate Commerce with foreign Nations, and among the several States, and with the Indian Tribes;

To establish an uniform Rule of Naturalization, and uniform Laws on the subject of Bankruptcies throughout the United States;

To coin Money, regulate the Value thereof, and of foreign Coin, and fix the Standard of Weights and Measures;

To provide for the Punishment of counterfeiting the Securities and current Coin of the United States;

To establish Post Offices and post Roads;

To promote the Progress of Science and useful Arts, by securing for limited Times to Authors and Inventors the exclusive Right to their respective Writings and Discoveries;

To constitute Tribunals inferior to the supreme Court;

To define and punish Piracies and Felonies committed on the high Seas, and offenses against the Law of Nations;

To declare War, grant Letters of Marque and Reprisal, and make Rules concerning Captures on Land and Water;

To raise and support Armies, but no Appropriation of Money to that Use shall be for a longer Term than two Years;

To provide and maintain a Navy;

To make Rules for the Government and Regulation of the land and naval Forces;

To provide for calling forth the Militia to execute the Laws of the Union, suppress Insurrections and repel Invasions;

To provide for organizing, arming, and disciplining, the Militia, and for governing such Part of them as may be employed in the Service of the United States, reserving to the States respectively, the Appointment of the Officers, and the Authority of training the Militia according to the discipline prescribed by Congress;

To exercise exclusive Legislation in all Cases whatsoever, over such District (not exceeding ten Miles square) as may, by Cession of particular States, and the Acceptance of Congress, become the Seat of the Government of the United States, and to exercise like Authority over all Places purchased by the Consent of the Legislature of the State in which the Same shall be, for the Erection of Forts, Magazines, Arsenals, dock-Yards, and other needful Buildings;—And

To make all Laws which shall be necessary and proper for carrying into Execution the foregoing Powers, and all other Powers vested by this Constitution in the Government of the United States, or in any Department or Officer thereof.

SECTION. 9.

The Migration or Importation of such Persons as any of the States now existing shall think proper to admit, shall not be prohibited by the Congress prior to the Year one thousand eight hundred and eight, but a Tax or duty may be imposed on such Importation, not exceeding ten dollars for each Person.

The Privilege of the Writ of Habeas Corpus shall not be suspended, unless when in Cases of Rebellion or Invasion the public Safety may require it.

No Bill of Attainder or ex post facto Law shall be passed.

No Capitation, or other direct, Tax shall be laid, unless in Proportion to the Census or enumeration herein before directed to be taken.

No Tax or Duty shall be laid on Articles exported from any State.

No Preference shall be given by any Regulation of Commerce or Revenue to the Ports of one State over those of another; nor shall Vessels bound to, or from, one State, be obliged to enter, clear, or pay Duties in another.

No Money shall be drawn from the Treasury, but in Consequence of Appropriations made by Law; and a regular Statement and Account of the Receipts and Expenditures of all public Money shall be published from time to time.

No Title of Nobility shall be granted by the United States: And no Person holding any Office of Profit or Trust under them, shall, without the Consent of the Congress, accept of any present, Emolument, Office, or Title, of any kind whatever, from any King, Prince, or foreign State.

SECTION. 10.

No State shall enter into any Treaty, Alliance, or Confederation; grant Letters of Marque and Reprisal; coin Money; emit Bills of Credit; make any Thing but gold and silver Coin a Tender in Payment of Debts; pass any Bill of Attainder, ex post facto Law, or Law impairing the Obligation of Contracts, or grant any Title of Nobility.

No State shall, without the Consent of the Congress, lay any Imposts or Duties on Imports or Exports, except what may be absolutely necessary for executing its inspection Laws: and the net Produce of all Duties and Imposts, laid by any State on Imports or Exports, shall be for the Use of the Treasury of the United States; and all such Laws shall be subject to the Revision and Control of the Congress.

No State shall, without the Consent of Congress, lay any Duty of Tonnage, keep Troops, or Ships of War in time of Peace, enter into any Agreement or Compact with another State, or with a foreign Power, or engage in War, unless actually invaded, or in such imminent Danger as will not admit of delay.

ARTICLE. II.

SECTION. 1.

The executive Power shall be vested in a President of the United States of America. He shall hold his Office during the Term of four Years, and, together with the Vice

President, chosen for the same Term, be elected, as follows: Each State shall appoint, in such Manner as the Legislature thereof may direct, a Number of Electors, equal to the whole Number of Senators and Representatives to which the State may be entitled in the Congress: but no Senator or Representative, or Person holding an Office of Trust or Profit under the United States, shall be appointed an Elector. The Electors shall meet in their respective States, and vote by Ballot for two Persons, of whom one at least shall not be an Inhabitant of the same State with themselves. And they shall make a List of all the Persons voted for, and of the Number of Votes for each; which List they shall sign and certify, and transmit sealed to the Seat of the Government of the United States, directed to the President of the Senate. The President of the Senate shall, in the Presence of the Senate and House of Representatives, open all the Certificates, and the Votes shall then be counted. The Person having the greatest Number of Votes shall be the President, if such Number be a Majority of the whole Number of Electors appointed; and if there be more than one who have such Majority, and have an equal Number of Votes, then the House of Representatives shall immediately choose by Ballot one of them for President; and if no Person have a Majority, then from the five highest on the List the said House shall in like Manner choose the President. But in choosing the President, the Votes shall be taken by States, the Representation from each State having one Vote; A quorum for this purpose shall consist of a Member or Members from two thirds of the States, and a Majority of all the States shall be necessary to a Choice. In every Case, after the Choice of the President, the Person having the greatest Number of Votes of the Electors shall be the Vice President. But if there should remain two or more who have equal

Votes, the Senate shall choose from them by Ballot the Vice President.

The Congress may determine the Time of choosing the Electors, and the Day on which they shall give their Votes; which Day shall be the same throughout the United States. No Person except a natural born Citizen, or a Citizen of the United States, at the time of the Adoption of this Constitution, shall be eligible to the Office of President; neither shall any Person be eligible to that Office who shall not have attained to the Age of thirty five Years, and been fourteen Years a Resident within the United States.

In Case of the Removal of the President from Office, or of his Death, Resignation, or Inability to discharge the Powers and Duties of the said Office, the Same shall devolve on the Vice President, and the Congress may by Law provide for the Case of Removal, Death, Resignation or Inability, both of the President and Vice President, declaring what Officer shall then act as President, and such Officer shall act accordingly, until the Disability be removed, or a President shall be elected.

The President shall, at stated Times, receive for his Services, a Compensation, which shall neither be increased nor diminished during the Period for which he shall have been elected, and he shall not receive within that Period any other Emolument from the United States, or any of them.

Before he enter on the Execution of his Office, he shall take the following Oath or Affirmation:— "I do solemnly swear (or affirm) that I will faithfully execute the Office of President of the United States, and will to the best of my Ability, preserve, protect and defend the Constitution of the United States."

SECTION. 2.

The President shall be Commander in Chief of the Army and Navy of the United States, and of the Militia of the several States, when called into the actual Service of the United States; he may require the Opinion, in writing, of the principal Officer in each of the executive Departments, upon any Subject relating to the Duties of their respective Offices, and he shall have Power to grant Reprieves and Pardons for offenses against the United States, except in Cases of Impeachment.

He shall have Power, by and with the Advice and Consent of the Senate, to make Treaties, provided two thirds of the Senators present concur; and he shall nominate, and by and with the Advice and Consent of the Senate, shall appoint Ambassadors, other public Ministers and Consuls, Judges of the supreme Court, and all other Officers of the United States, whose Appointments are not herein otherwise provided for, and which shall be established by Law: but the Congress may by Law vest the Appointment of such inferior Officers, as they think proper, in the President alone, in the Courts of Law, or in the Heads of Departments.

The President shall have Power to fill up all Vacancies that may happen during the Recess of the Senate, by granting Commissions which shall expire at the End of their next Session.

SECTION. 3.

He shall from time to time give to the Congress Information of the State of the Union, and recommend to their Consideration such Measures as he shall judge necessary and expedient; he may, on extraordinary Occasions, convene both

Houses, or either of them, and in Case of Disagreement between them, with Respect to the Time of Adjournment, he may adjourn them to such Time as he shall think proper; he shall receive Ambassadors and other public Ministers; he shall take Care that the Laws be faithfully executed, and shall Commission all the Officers of the United States.

SECTION. 4.
The President, Vice President and all civil Officers of the United States, shall be removed from Office on Impeachment for, and Conviction of, Treason, Bribery, or other high Crimes and Misdemeanors.

ARTICLE III.

SECTION. 1.
The judicial Power of the United States shall be vested in one supreme Court, and in such inferior Courts as the Congress may from time to time ordain and establish. The Judges, both of the supreme and inferior Courts, shall hold their Offices during good Behavior, and shall, at stated Times, receive for their Services a Compensation, which shall not be diminished during their Continuance in Office.

SECTION. 2.
The judicial Power shall extend to all Cases, in Law and Equity, arising under this Constitution, the Laws of the United States, and Treaties made, or which shall be made, under their Authority;—to all Cases affecting Ambassadors, other public Ministers and Consuls;—to all Cases of admiralty and maritime Jurisdiction;—to Controversies to which the United States shall be a Party;—to Controversies

between two or more States;— between a State and Citizens of another State;—between Citizens of different States;— between Citizens of the same State claiming Lands under Grants of different States, and between a State, or the Citizens thereof, and foreign States, Citizens or Subjects.

In all Cases affecting Ambassadors, other public Ministers and Consuls, and those in which a State shall be Party, the supreme Court shall have original Jurisdiction. In all the other Cases before mentioned, the supreme Court shall have appellate Jurisdiction, both as to Law and Fact, with such Exceptions, and under such Regulations as the Congress shall make.

The Trial of all Crimes, except in Cases of Impeachment, shall be by Jury; and such Trial shall be held in the State where the said Crimes shall have been committed; but when not committed within any State, the Trial shall be at such Place or Places as the Congress may by Law have directed.

SECTION. 3.

Treason against the United States, shall consist only in levying War against them, or in adhering to their Enemies, giving them Aid and Comfort. No Person shall be convicted of Treason unless on the Testimony of two Witnesses to the same overt Act, or on Confession in open Court.

The Congress shall have Power to declare the Punishment of Treason, but no Attainder of Treason shall work Corruption of Blood, or Forfeiture except during the Life of the Person attainted.

ARTICLE. IV.

SECTION. 1.
Full Faith and Credit shall be given in each State to the public Acts, Records, and judicial Proceedings of every other State. And the Congress may by general Laws prescribe the Manner in which such Acts, Records and Proceedings shall be proved, and the Effect thereof.

SECTION. 2.
The Citizens of each State shall be entitled to all Privileges and Immunities of Citizens in the several States.

A Person charged in any State with Treason, Felony, or other Crime, who shall flee from Justice, and be found in another State, shall on Demand of the executive Authority of the State from which he fled, be delivered up, to be removed to the State having Jurisdiction of the Crime.

No Person held to Service or Labour in one State, under the Laws thereof, escaping into another, shall, in Consequence of any Law or Regulation therein, be discharged from such Service or Labour, but shall be delivered up on Claim of the Party to whom such Service or Labour may be due.

SECTION. 3.
New States may be admitted by the Congress into this Union; but no new State shall be formed or erected within the Jurisdiction of any other State; nor any State be formed by the Junction of two or more States, or Parts of States, without the Consent of the Legislatures of the States concerned as well as of the Congress.

The Congress shall have Power to dispose of and make all needful Rules and Regulations respecting the Territory or other Property belonging to the United States; and nothing in this Constitution shall be so construed as to Prejudice any Claims of the United States, or of any particular State.

SECTION. 4.

The United States shall guarantee to every State in this Union a Republican Form of Government, and shall protect each of them against Invasion; and on Application of the Legislature, or of the Executive (when the Legislature cannot be convened), against domestic Violence.

ARTICLE. V.

The Congress, whenever two thirds of both Houses shall deem it necessary, shall propose Amendments to this Constitution, or, on the Application of the Legislatures of two thirds of the several States, shall call a Convention for proposing Amendments, which, in either Case, shall be valid to all Intents and Purposes, as Part of this Constitution, when ratified by the Legislatures of three fourths of the several States, or by Conventions in three fourths thereof, as the one or the other Mode of Ratification may be proposed by the Congress; Provided that no Amendment which may be made prior to the Year One thousand eight hundred and eight shall in any Manner affect the first and fourth Clauses in the Ninth Section of the first Article; and that no State, without its Consent, shall be deprived of its equal Suffrage in the Senate.

ARTICLE. VI.

All Debts contracted and Engagements entered into, before

the Adoption of this Constitution, shall be as valid against the United States under this Constitution, as under the Confederation.

This Constitution, and the Laws of the United States which shall be made in Pursuance thereof; and all Treaties made, or which shall be made, under the Authority of the United States, shall be the supreme Law of the Land; and the Judges in every State shall be bound thereby, any Thing in the Constitution or Laws of any State to the Contrary notwithstanding.

The Senators and Representatives before mentioned, and the Members of the several State Legislatures, and all executive and judicial Officers, both of the United States and of the several States, shall be bound by Oath or Affirmation, to support this Constitution; but no religious Test shall ever be required as a Qualification to any Office or public Trust under the United States.

ARTICLE. VII.

The Ratification of the Conventions of nine States, shall be sufficient for the Establishment of this Constitution between the States so ratifying the Same.

The Word, "the," being interlined between the seventh and eighth Lines of the first Page, the Word "Thirty" being partly written on an Erasure in the fifteenth Line of the first Page, The Words "is tried" being interlined between the thirty second and thirty third Lines of the first Page and the Word "the" being interlined between the forty third and forty fourth Lines of the second Page.

Attest William Jackson Secretary

Done in Convention by the Unanimous Consent of the States present the Seventeenth Day of September in the Year of our Lord one thousand seven hundred and Eighty seven and of the Independence of the United States of America the Twelfth In witness whereof We have hereunto subscribed our Names,

The Bill of Rights

The Bill of Rights consists of the first 10 amendments to the United States Constitution. These amendments limit the powers of the federal government, protecting the rights of all citizens, residents and visitors on United States territory. Among the enumerated rights these amendments guarantee are: the freedoms of speech, press, and religion; the people's right to keep and bear arms; the freedom of assembly; the freedom to petition; and the rights to be free of unreasonable search and seizure; cruel and unusual punishment; and compelled self-incrimination. The Bill of Rights also restricts Congress' power by prohibiting it from making any law respecting establishment of religion and by prohibiting the federal government from depriving any person of life, liberty, or property without due process of law. In criminal cases, it requires indictment by grand jury for any capital or "infamous crime," guarantees a speedy public trial with an impartial and local jury, and prohibits double jeopardy. In addition, the Bill of Rights states that "the enumeration in the Constitution, of certain rights, shall not be construed to deny or disparage others retained by the people,"[1] and reserves all powers not granted to the Federal government to the citizenry or States.

These amendments came into effect on December 15, 1791, when ratified by three-fourths of the States. Most were applied to the states by a series of decisions applying the due process clause of the Fourteenth Amendment, which was adopted after the American Civil War.

Initially drafted by James Madison in 1789, the Bill of Rights was written at a time when ideological conflict between Federalists and anti-Federalists, dating from the Philadelphia Convention in 1787, threatened the Constitution's ratification. The Bill was influenced by George Mason's 1776 Virginia Declaration of Rights, the 1689 English Bill of Rights, works of the Age of Enlightenment pertaining to natural rights, and earlier English political documents such as Magna Carta (1215). The Bill was largely a response to the Constitution's influential opponents, including prominent Founding Fathers, who argued that it failed to protect the basic principles of human liberty.

The Bill of Rights plays a central role in American law and government, and remains a fundamental symbol of the freedoms and culture of the nation. One of the original fourteen copies of the Bill of Rights is on public display at the National Archives in Washington, D.C.

The Bill of Rights: A Transcription
The Preamble to The Bill of Rights

Congress of the United States
begun and held at the City of New-York, on
Wednesday the fourth of March, one thousand seven hundred and eighty nine.

THE Conventions of a number of the States, having at the time of their adopting the Constitution, expressed a desire, in order to prevent misconstruction or abuse of its powers, that further declaratory and restrictive clauses should be added: And as extending the ground of public confidence in the Government, will best ensure the beneficent ends of its institution.

RESOLVED by the Senate and House of Representatives of the United States of America, in Congress assembled, two thirds of both Houses concurring, that the following Articles be proposed to the Legislatures of the several States, as amendments to the Constitution of the United States, all, or any of which Articles, when ratified by three fourths of the said Legislatures, to be valid to all intents and purposes, as part of the said Constitution; viz.

ARTICLES in addition to, and Amendment of the Constitution of the United States of America, proposed by Congress, and ratified by the Legislatures of the several States, pursuant to the fifth Article of the original Constitution.

Note: The following text is a transcription of the first ten amendments to the Constitution in their original form. These amendments were ratified December 15, 1791, and form what is known as the "Bill of Rights."

Amendment I

Congress shall make no law respecting an establishment of religion, or prohibiting the free exercise thereof; or abridging the freedom of speech, or of the press; or the right of the people peaceably to assemble, and to petition the Government for a redress of grievances.

Amendment II

A well regulated Militia, being necessary to the security of a free State, the right of the people to keep and bear Arms, shall not be infringed.

Amendment III
No Soldier shall, in time of peace be quartered in any house, without the consent of the Owner, nor in time of war, but in a manner to be prescribed by law.

Amendment IV
The right of the people to be secure in their persons, houses, papers, and effects, against unreasonable searches and seizures, shall not be violated, and no Warrants shall issue, but upon probable cause, supported by Oath or affirmation, and particularly describing the place to be searched, and the persons or things to be seized.

Amendment V
No person shall be held to answer for a capital, or otherwise infamous crime, unless on a presentment or indictment of a Grand Jury, except in cases arising in the land or naval forces, or in the Militia, when in actual service in time of War or public danger; nor shall any person be subject for the same offense to be twice put in jeopardy of life or limb; nor shall be compelled in any criminal case to be a witness against himself, nor be deprived of life, liberty, or property, without due process of law; nor shall private property be taken for public use, without just compensation.

Amendment VI
In all criminal prosecutions, the accused shall enjoy the right to a speedy and public trial, by an impartial jury of the State and district wherein the crime shall have been committed, which district shall have been previously ascertained by law, and to be informed of the nature and cause of the accusation; to be confronted with the witnesses against him; to have

compulsory process for obtaining witnesses in his favor, and to have the Assistance of Counsel for his Defense.

Amendment VII

In Suits at common law, where the value in controversy shall exceed twenty dollars, the right of trial by jury shall be preserved, and no fact tried by a jury, shall be otherwise re-examined in any Court of the United States, than according to the rules of the common law.

Amendment VIII

Excessive bail shall not be required, nor excessive fines imposed, nor cruel and unusual punishments inflicted.

Amendment IX

The enumeration in the Constitution, of certain rights, shall not be construed to deny or disparage others retained by the people.

Amendment X

The powers not delegated to the United States by the Constitution, nor prohibited by it to the States, are reserved to the States respectively, or to the people.

About the Author

George Cappannelli is the CEO of AgeNation, a new multi-platform media company dedicated to redefining what it means to live consciously and age wisely in the 21st Century. He also leads The Information and Training Company, the business consulting and training organization he founded 22 years ago.

He is a leading expert in individual, organizational and societal change and has extensive experience in both the public and private sectors. Under the banner of The Information and Training Company his clients include a number of Fortune 500 companies, government agencies and national associations: Accenture, The Boeing Company, Hughes Space & Communications, TRW, PepsiCo, NASA, Taco Bell, Pacific Bell, Sun Microsystems, Honeywell, National Oceanographic Aeronautics Administration (NOAA), Oracle, Space Systems/Loral, The National Forest Service, Grumman, The U.S. Navy, The U.S. Postal Service, The Walt Disney Company, The Israel Government,The Los Angeles Times, and many others.

In addition to his work in the corporate sector and his new work on conscious living and wise aging under the auspices of AgeNation, he has had a very diverse career. He has been privileged to work with a number of world leaders including: Desmond Tutu, Lech Wallesa, Golda Meir, Mother Teresa and The Dalai Lama. As President and Founder of two New York based film and television production companies, Theater Visions and Axial Productions, his work won a number of International Film Awards, as well as ANDY, CLEO and two special category EMMY Awards.

He was Co-Founder and Director of The Institute for Individual and World Peace and The International Integrity Program, served as Executive Director of The Sedona Institute and as one of the Directors of The Society for the Advancement of Human Spirit, an organization chaired by The Dalai Lama.

He served as a lead facilitator for Insight Seminars and was a member of the group that founded The Insight Consulting Group. His background also includes work in the advertising and marketing field where he served as Executive Vice President and Creative Director of Allerton, Berman and Dean, A New York firm.

In 1991 he returned to the political arena where he managed a U.S. Senate Campaign in California. He also served as a special consultant in the 1992 presidential campaign and in 2004 served as the chief strategist in a mayoral campaign that elected the first democrat in 30 years by the largest plurality in the town's history.

Mr. Cappannelli is a well-known key note speaker as well as an award winning sculptor whose works in stone, wood and bronze are in a number of public and private collections. As a writer his books include: *"Say Yes to Change" (Walking Stick Press 2002)*, *"Authenticity (Emmis, 2004), It's About Time (Onlife, 2001)* and *Making The Best of The Rest of Your Life. (Due out this Fall.)* He is also the author of two new novels entitled *"Old Stones & Promises"* and *"Life After Life."*

He resides in Santa Fe with his wife Sedena who is one of his business partners as well as co-author of *Say Yes to Change, Authenticity,* and *Making the Best of the Rest of Your Life.*

Praise for the Author's Work

"Purpose and meaning is a very important subject explored in voices that have been there and know the ground. The Cappannelli's are the real deal. Their coaching work with world class organizations and high performing individuals gets to the heart of the matter and, in the end, it is certainly the heart that matters when dealing with the subject of meaning and purpose."

Melina Borrows, Contributing Writer
at Cosmopolitan & Ladies Home Journal

"In these turbulent times we are all faced with dramatic changes. Our ability to accept change, to deal with it consciously and with the kind of optimism, positive attitude and confidence that George & Sedena Cappannelli discuss in this book may well be one of the most important abilities we can develop. That, of course, and our constant focus on love which in the end is the most important antidote we have against the fear that limits us."

Gerald Jampolski, Author of <u>Love Is Letting Go of Fear</u>

"In a world as technologically advanced as ours, it is easy to get overwhelmed by change. Yet change, as George & Sedena Cappannelli remind us in this book, is not only inevitable but valuable. The unique insights and practical tools they share with us can help us – as executive teams and as individuals to live more expansive, empowered and successful lives."

Brewster Shaw, US Astronaut and Boeing's
Director of The Manned Flight

"It is clear that our world is changing at an astounding rate and that every aspect of our lives and every segment of our culture is effected by this change. What is not yet clear is how well or quickly our society as a whole will adapt to this change. In the Cultural Creatives we identified an important and growing segment that we believe are not only ready for change, but committed to making it positive. We are sure that many of the Cultural Creatives will find value in Say Yes To Change. It offers some unique insights and some very practical wisdom that can help us make change our ally."

Paul H. Ray, Author of The Cultural Creatives

"This is a terrific book for our times! George and Sedena Cappannelli are "truth-tellers" and in Authenticity they have given us a gem of a book. Their keen insights, spiritual wisdom and practical advice challenge and invite us to live a richer, deeper life of meaning and inner integrity. I strongly recommend it to people of faith everywhere."

The Very Reverend Edward H. Harrison,
Dean, St. John's Cathedral

"Authenticity is a thought-provoking journey into the real art of leadership and I recommend it to anyone aspiring to positively influence others and to empower their own lives. It is a unique resource for identifying integrity at the most basic level – the level of one's meaning and purpose in life."

Rhodes Robinson, CEO, Environmental Services Inc.

Participate in the Next Phase of The American Revolution!

Dear Reader

Thank you for taking the time to read **I Dream Of A New America**. If you resonate with some of the ideas and concepts presented here and believe that it is time for us to take greater responsibility for our own governance and to reclaim the legacy of this great democracy, please contact us.

I believe that by working together we can identify new solutions to some of the major challenges we face and bring stronger vision, greater compassion, cooperation and collaboration back into the day by day business of making democracy work. I also believe that together, acting in good faith and with greater consciousness, we can act on the principles and core values articulated by our founding fathers and turn this ship of state on a heading toward a positive, sane and sustainable future.

So join me online at www.IDreamOfANewAmerica.com. You can share your ideas, interact with others who have common interests, and learn about different ways you can get involved in making a difference. You will also find special digital copies of the I Dream of America Prologue and The Open Letter To A Political Candidate that you can share with your friends and associates.

If you are also interested in learning more about how you can live consciously and age wisely and make a difference in the 21st Century, please visit us at: www.AgeNation.com

In the spirit of a new tomorrow,

George Cappannelli

To order a FREE catalog call 800-729-4131 or visit www.nohoax.com

www.ingramcontent.com/pod-product-compliance
Lightning Source LLC
Chambersburg PA
CBHW072120270326
41931CB00010B/1618